Women's Movement in Manipur

About the Author

Dr Th. Binarani Devi hailing from professional family obtained her degrees of M.Phil. and Ph.D. from Department of Political Science, Manipur University under the supervision of Prof. Ksh. Bimola Devi former Dean, School of Social, Science. Presently she is working as Senior Lecturer in Department of Political Science, G.P Women's College, Imphal. She has published twelve articles and completed a major research project under University Grants Commission, New Delhi.

Women's Movement in Manipur

Thokchom Binarani Devi

CONCEPT PUBLISHING COMPANY PVT. LTD.
NEW DELHI-110059

ISBN-13 : 978-81-8069-779-1

First Published 2011

Published and Printed by

Concept
Since 1974

Concept Publishing Company Pvt. Ltd.
Regd. Office:
A/15-16, Commercial Block, Mohan Garden
New Delhi-110059 (India)
Phones : 25351460, 25351794, *Fax* : 091-11-25357109
Email : publishing@conceptpub.com
Website: www.conceptpub.com

Editorial Office:
H-13, Bali Nagar, New Delhi-110 015, India

Cataloging in Publication Data--*Courtesy:* D.K. Agencies (P) Ltd. <docinfo@dkagencies.com>

Binarani Devi, Thokchom.
Women's movement in Manipur / Thokchom Binarani Devi.
p. cm.
Includes bibliographical references (p.) and index.
ISBN 9788180697791

1. Feminism—India—Manipur. 2. Women—India—Manipur—Social conditions. 3. Women—India—Manipur—Economic conditions. 4. Pressure groups—India—Manipur. 5. Women—Political activity—India—Manipur. I. Title.

DDC 305.42095417 22

Dedicated
To

MY GRAND PARENTS

(who cared and encouraged me all the time)

Foreword

The study on women has become a very important academic pursuit since the middle of 1970s. The growth and development of a democratic society based on equality, liberty, freedom and welfare programmes largely depends on the participation of women in the democratic process of the state. Women who were subjected to various kinds of subordination and inferiority position due to traditional social norms, beliefs and practices, handed down from generation to generation depicting gender roles are called for to empower themselves from within and from the laws , enactments, policies framed by the government. Though active in social and economic activities, women found themselves trapped in the traditional social jurisdiction. Democracy promised them the enjoyment of equal political rights with men as candidates as well as voters in the electoral process and equal participation in the decision making process of the state. But in all democratic countries of the world, women participating in the decision making process are found to be less than men. The question is how this happens after so many covenants, conventions, passed by the United Nations making women equal with men as individuals since 1948 and the democratic countries guaranteeing equal political rights with men in their respective constitutions. There still exists a big gap between what is written in the constitutions and various laws passed by the democratic countries and what is prevailing in practice. Of course, the equality of women with men cannot be achieved as easily as the inequality is firmly rooted in the society before the outbreak of the French Revolution, 1789.

It is interesting to note that even famous sociologists Augustus Comte, Max Weber etc. very often described women as domestic. Women were not considered as members of the society. Society means only men (excluding women). The discussion and correspondence between Max Weber and Merianm Weber's idea that women possess equal "intellectual capacity" like men. Max Weber only advised Marianm Weber not encompass the "intellectual area" by women but to discover new area within the domestic jurisdiction which men cannot interfere. Such is long history of women's movement, nearly more than two centuries. It was only after the Second World War that women issues had become important areas for the development of the democratic societies. The political equality guaranteed by the democratic constitutions in the form of fundamental rights, political rights etc. is not able to penetrate deeply in the social roots in spite of many policies and programmes of the government. In the beginning of this 21st century, women issues are still facing many challenges from the social and economic sectors.

It is against this socio-economic and political background of the society that Dr. Th. Binarani Devi has taken up women's issues and their larger perspectives in a democratic country. The democratic government has also a great responsibility to create favourable socio-economic and political atmosphere for the empowerment of women, making them capable citizens of the state to discharge their duties in a positive and rightful manner. The issue of governance may be considered as more important than others for the creation of rightful and conducive atmosphere, not only for women themselves but also for the society at large. It is in this context that Dr. Binarani emphasized on a functional and effective democracy. If not satisfied with the functioning of the government and governance, the people, in groups, have every right to correct the wrongdoings of the government through movements. The role of the pressure groups in the pluralistic society as a link between the people and the government focussed and emphasized. The pressure groups always check the working of the democratic government by highlighting the wrong doings and the negative aspects of administration and governance.

The emergence of women's organizations as pressure groups is of recent phenomenon. But in Manipur, the history of women's groups, though not organized formally, but acting as pressure groups, can be traced as early as the time of the monarchy i.e, during the British period. It might be due to historical reasons of having Lallup system (every adult male member from every family working in the palace ten days out of forty) and accompanying the king in his frequent warfare against the neighbouring rulers etc. made the womenfolk aware of the social, economic and political matters, which had affected their families. So, the womenfolk as a collective force could even correct the wrong doings as well as the mistake committed in the administrative and political aspects.

The author further examines in depth the working and role of women voluntary organizations of all sections of the population, such as the Meiteis, the Nagas, the Kukis, and the Manipuri Muslims (Meitei Pangals), after the merger of Manipur into the Indian Union, 1949. The book is an important source of information regarding the working of women's organizations and the impact on the democratic process in Manipur.

I wish Dr. Th. Binarani Devi all success in this important endeavour and more in her future life. Being herself acquainted in this area for many years and being exposed herself in the field, as a research scholar by presenting papers, to various seminars, conferences and meets, the book will certainly benefit the serious scholars, students and those who are sincere in tracing out women's movements in Manipur in particular. I congratulate her once again on this important feat she has achieved in this area.

Dr. Ksh. Bimola Devi

Preface

Women organizations are so important in a multi-cultural, multi-lingual, and multi-religious plural society. As women constitute nearly half of the total population, their share and contributions cannot be neglected. If this section of population is not counted any research work in the field of social science will be an incomplete one. The purpose of a democratic society is the welfare and development of the whole society. As well as the contribution of the members of the whole society is the only means which we can get the purpose of a democratic society.

When the woman is a single, she cannot express her own problems, ambitions, needs etc. Mainly in a society where strict traditional social norms are inheriting by the members of the society, it is very difficult and problematic for a woman to come out from the strict social norms and adjust with this modern liberalized global world. The practical realities of women's work and interests, than, as well as the fulfilment of the more abstract liberating potential of women's activism require that our politics built from recognition is a far cry from its glorification. It acknowledges women's traditional association with reproduction and its values in the very moment of denying the necessity or inevitability of that special relationship, and refusing the oppression that it has institutionalized. It brings the specific perspective of women to the age old struggle of 'man' against domination, and in doing so posits a revolutionary affirmation and transformation of both radicalism and women's specificity, feminism articulates new and more universal truths— truths which end narrow single sex definitions of the world, and in the process, feminism and humanized politics.

The power and powerlessness of the women made up a changing cycle, depending on the status of her husband, her possession of son, her fertility, looks, health and capacity for domestic labour. Traditional progressive values such as equality, dignity and freedom are central to women's struggle, but to limit the conceptualization of our politics to these existing parameters is to deny its deeper revolutionary implication. Feminist's politics must extend earlier progressive values in ways that reflect the transforming presence of women on the political stage. We are not simply entering politics as it has existed. When fully half of the human race has been excluded from the practice and definition of politics, our entry necessarily transformed its very shape and definition. Women's entry into politics as women is, in fact, the emergence of the long subordinate, devalued and marginalized sphere of private life and reproduction into the public and is an event of world historical significance.

The women's issue can be adequately addressed only through social movements both at the regional and national levels. The national and state commissions for women cannot be expected to do much because they function under the authority of the state which in turn operates under the dictates of international organizations that are least bothered with the women's issues. At present women do not even enjoy the basic rights enshrined in the Constitution. In India, women activism is registered in the historical struggle for nationalism, worker's right and present struggles. In the North East Region of India the women have a rich history of movements in the insurgency affected areas. The collective empowerment and organized movements for common cause is the need of the day. The collective movement of such nature requires not only organization at the local level but also need network organizations at the national and international levels. Women's movement could countervail the state power. There is a real need to show organizational strength for making the state take proactive role in favour of women. Insensitive way in which the state addresses movements was also seen when a case of attempted suicide was lodged against the raising of the level of Narmada Dam. The women's movement challenges the police and judiciary primarily as patriarchal structure of power and reshapes the potential of a powerful community of women who would in turn be tied against an unjust social order. This applies the North East too and the women's movement in the region needs to become also a part of similar movement at the national level. We should remind ourselves that compartmentalization of issues of concern should not be carried too far. Very often the issues of women also implicate the children and the young people. The displaced men and women are very closely related. Hence women's movement ought to be coordinated with all the similar movements that aim at securing equal rights of men and women.

The participation of women in popular mass movements goes without saying, particularly in the North-Eastern India where women are more actively involved in economic and social activities. One of the prime contributions of the women's movement is solidarity which transcends barriers of race, locally, caste and to some extent class also. These differences are huge but a major premise of the women rooted as it is in the patriarchal structure of society which is also ultimately responsible for the caste and class system. In the North-Eastern India women are forced to be subordinate both from external pressure of the men-folk to comfort to the community norms as well as due to lack of self-confidence. This may sound paradoxical in the North-Eastern India, in states like Meghalaya and Manipur whose women are economically and educationally advanced. But in fact there is a strong tradition barring women's participation in politics in both these states which consequently have a poor showing of women even in conventional electoral politics. There have been strong women's movements for instance in the Nupilal Movements and later the anti-liquor and anti-drug movements (Nisha Bandh) in Manipur but these have been primarily social rather than political in nature, without a modern sense of political identity. After the accession of Manipur to the Indian Union, the women community once again energized their role in the struggle for restoration of democracy and fought against the Undemocratic Advisory Council (1952-53), the Territorial Council, and finally fought for the movement for statehood. The tradition of Meitei women's powerful civil society organizations rising against oppressive measures of the state and also against social evils is quite evident even today. In recent times they have been agitating against the Armed Forces Special Power Act operating in Manipur. The activities of women in groups or as members of voluntary organizations or non-governmental organizations, pressure groups have a forceful impact on the political process of the state.

The whole book is divided into six chapters. The first chapter is 'Introduction'. In this present day socio- economic and political conditions of Manipur, the role of the voluntary organizations or associations as a pressure group is very important. The increasing discontent of the people, repeated failure of crops, the steep devaluation of the rupee, pressure from foreign governments, mounting bribery and corruption, the havoc created by casteism, linguism and regionalism etc. put democracy on a trial in India. In an underdeveloped society like Manipur, where there is a big question on the functional process of democracy and its effectiveness, the immediate needs is of a free society of free man— which is a basic necessity of a functional and effective democracy. Really it is a big hurdle, a fierce and dangerous battle which can only be fought with the culture of peace.

When the people are not satisfied with the decision and policies of the government, which is unsuitable to the public, they formally complain to the government. If the government does not consider or take into account the complaint, then the affected persons along with others can protest or even call strike against the government. Thus the people can curb the wrongful activities of the government. Protest and strikes may in course of time develop into a form of political movement with the help of the mass media. The degree of political participation of the people increased in the socio-political movement through the activities of pressure group. In this chapter, the exact picture of the whole book is trying to depict, including the objectives of the study, methodology, review of the related literature and the importance of the study.

The second chapter is titled with 'Meaning and Role of Pressure Groups in a Democratic Society'. All the countries of the world are adopting or trying to adopt democratic form of government, which may be direct or indirect. Political participation in a democracy derives from the principle of equal rights and achieving the best in public welfare, and since there is no objective way of determining which particular individual might most acceptably discover and utter them, all are entitle to formulate their opinions with equal rights. This political equality gives the maximum encouragement to criticism of public official keeping them to aware of popular needs, and desires and obliging them to answer. Present day society is pluralistic and dynamic. It consists of many vocational, religious, ethnic, linguistic, economic, cultural and other groups, each having particular interests, aims and aspirations. When any of these groups tries to bring any pressure on any branch of government, it becomes a pressure group. Whether the groups exerting pressure on government are good or bad depends upon the manner in which they function. If their activities are purposeful and wholesome, pressure groups form a good link between the people and the government and aid in the democratic processes. These things are clearly explained in this chapter.

'Women's Organization and Pressure Groups in Manipur, is the third chapter. This chapter starts with the position and role of women in individual and groups in different parts of the world generally and especially in Manipur— pre and post-merger with the Indian Union. The problems faced by the women due to different social norms and realities are shown clearly in this chapter. As a result of patriarchal social norms, women were facing different gendered problems. But within the midst of gender inequality and gender differences women were contributing a lot to the socio-economic and political activities of the state. Different women's movements before the merger of Manipur to the Indian Union like Nupi Lal First of 1904; Nupi Lal Second of 1939 are clearly explained here. This chapter clearly discussed about the activities of women groups and their relationship with the imminent leaders and frontal organizations before the signing of the Merger Agreement. The activities of these women were even making a different feeling to the mighty British Empire, and it was a difficult task to control the movement of women in Manipur for them. The Nationalist leaders also tried to interpret the cause of the women's movement as a harbinger for Nationalism in the state. One can proudly say that the real feelings of nationalism to the people of Manipur were instilled by the women during the period of British Imperialism. The actions of the movement, for them, may not be the true sense of nationalism. But the idea behind the movement founded the true colour of nationalism to all the people of the state.

The fourth chapter is dealing with the women's movement of Manipur after signing the merger agreement in 1949, titled with 'Women's Organization and Women's Movement after the Merger Agreement (1949)'. When Manipur became a part of the Indian Union in 1949, the socio-political and economic conditions of Manipur invited the formation of different voluntary organizations in the state. The importance of such voluntary organizations came to acknowledge by the people of all the communities who are residing in the state. The typical different nature of Manipuri women is highlighted here. The different women organizations of different communities like All Manipur Nupi Marup, Social Reformation and Development Samaj, Kuki Mother's Association, Kuki Women Human Rights Network, Ushoipokpi Tharaorok Women's Organization (Muslim) etc. are performing different activities for socio-political and economic development of the state by resolving all the conflict situations which are happening from time to time. For achieving their goals they are giving different forms of pressures to the government which the existing government could not remain in silent. The outcome of the movement may be slow or delayed but the relentless efforts of the women's organizations in collaboration with different frontal organizations are very difficult to neglect by the existing government.

Fifth chapter of this book is "Impact of Women's Organization in a Democratic Society". In the beginning of this chapter I am trying to focus about the problems and hindrances in connection with the establishment and implementation of the real meaning of democracy in the developing third world countries. The position of women in connection with work and time allocations; their educational status; impact of globalization etc. are clearly discussed here because it has a great impact in the slow progress of women empowerment. Even though they are facing a lot of difficulties and challenges, they are not remained in silent. They are struggling in group or even individual. When they are united and grouped they have a great fantastic role in the socio-economic and political development of the whole society. Their activities are not confined with the issues of women. The main target of this chapter is about the contribution of women in the development and progress of a democratic society.

The last chapter, Chapter VI is the Conclusion. Women are as active as a member and leader of civil society organizations and with the pressure they are giving to the existing government, society can get the real fruits of democracy. They exhibit the real meaning of participatory democracy. But they are required to enhance their activities with proper legislations. The only surest means for this purpose is the political empowerment of women. The importance of political empowerment and why women are not so advance in party politics are also mentioned here.

Acknowledgements

I take this opportunity to express my sincere gratitude to my former College Principal (L) Dr. Karam Manimohan Sing, who encouraged me to take up the work and shaped it into a concrete one.

Next, I owe my profound debt to Prof. Ksh. Bimola Devi, former Dean, School of Social Sciences, Manipur University who was my supervisor in both M.Phil. and Ph.D. I am giving my thanks to my friends — Dr. K. Kunjani Devi, Nalini Nongmeikapam, Th. Premita Devi and junior friends— Seityabati Devi, Sharmila; and again, my colleagues Dr. Ninghorla Zimik, Gaipuiru Kamei and Lingjahat Kipgen; and others who inspired and helped me to articulate my views in producing this book. Again, next I am giving my thanks to those office bearers of different governmental and non-governmental organizations, especially women organizations who had given me all the information without any hesitation for this work.

Again, I am giving my sincere thanks to Concept Publishing Company Pvt. Ltd. for their kind acceptance for publishing this volume into a book form.

Last but not least, I am deeply indebted to my family members for their understanding and physical and moral support which have been a source of inspiration and perseverance throughout the whole period of the research work.

1st June 2009

TH. BINARANI DEVI

Sr. Lect. G.P. Women's College,

Imphal

Contents

1

Introduction

Modern democratic society is a pluralistic and egalitarian in which the individual has equal status with others. Under a democratic system of government the value and dignity of the human personality is recognized. Every individual is free to live in his own way, think freely, enjoy the company of people he likes and becomes a member of associations and parties of his choice. Not only in the political sphere, but in social and economic fields too the individuals enjoy complete freedom. But the basic doubt in the mind of the people of this society is whether there is a working democracy prevailing in the society or is it bringing about the desired end. This doubt is unfortunately not cleared most of the time which resulted in socio-political dissatisfaction among the people and which further increases the doubt and confusion. This increased confusion made by people with certain common sense, feel the need of a participatory democracy and modern women as very active member of today's society too, shared this feeling. A democratic society is one where the government and the citizens come together to create an open society where there is maximum and effective public participation. Citizen must evince an active interest in the formulation of policies and their execution and thus exercise their democratic rights as important stakeholders in the governance process.[1] Participatory democracy does not mean that all the people will necessarily take part in the decision making process.

Democratic society stands for an egalitarian society in which the individual has equal status with others. Social inequality has been a historical fact. Some people enjoyed the loaves and fishes, luxurious cloths and buildings and cloths, while others could hardly get a square meal a day, staying nights at the roadsides etc. The idea of equality was formulated with an eye of remaining such social injustice. With the development of democracy, it came to be accepted as a matter of principle that as a free legal agent in the scheme of the state, the legal personality of each individual is equal to that of every other. Equality, after all, is a derivative value. It is derived from the supreme value of the development of personality, in each alike and equality, but each along its own different line and of its own separate motion. Different prominent social scientists are giving full emphases on the doctrine of democracy. W. F. Willoughby clearly expressed this idea in his definition, "The word democracy is unfortunately used in popular discussion, and indeed in much political literature in two quite different senses: as designating a society or community in which class distinctions are absent or relatively unimportant, and as designating a distinct form of government."[2] The aim of democracy has everywhere been to eliminate man-made socially fostered, discrimination that has enlarged for some and restricted for others the avenues that lead to education, income and advancement. In a democracy, man or a group of man cannot rule as they please without the consent of the people, but the governmental machinery has to move according to the wishes of the people and for meeting the requirements of the people. Government has to be responsive to public opinion, and in the light of genuine and responsible public criticism it may have to change its course for the benefit of the people. An unpopular and inefficient government, which has lost the confidence of the people, is likely to be overthrown by the pressure of public criticism and through the ballot box. A democratic government is not a tool of oppression or an arbitrary tool of a few people, but machinery in which the representatives of the people act according to the wishes of the voters. It implies the right of free discussion and criticism to all the people, the right to form various parties and associations for propagating ideas freely, the freedom of the press, a liberal suffrage, periodical elections, absence of privileges, full enjoyment of liberties and equality before the law. In a democratic society non-political associations are allowed their liberty, equality, discussion, opposition and tolerance. In connection with this situation Robert A. Dahl clearly said that, "a democratic society is a social system that not only has democratic political (sub) system but also a number of other sub-systems that operates so as to contribute directly or indirectly to the strength of the democratic political processes".[3] Mainly in a democratic political system input function is performed by the society in the form of demand and support. While the organs of the government remain silent without giving any response to the input function, the society needs to give pressure to the government by highlighting about the issue conditionally. Thus, there can be multifarious pressure groups which organize themselves under efficient leadership. Whether the groups exerting pressure on government are good or bad depends upon the manner in which they functioned. If their activities are purposeful and wholesome, pressure group form a good link between the people the Government and aid in the democratic processes.

Statement of the Problem

The existence of the pluralistic type of society in modern time means the presence as well as the relevance of the innumerable variables and their proper representation. The formal structure as well as the party system proved inadequate. On the other hand, a third approach of unofficial power has come into existence. The study of pressure group, also known as the interest, organized and catalytic groups, within the conceptual framework constitutes an interesting as well as important part of the study of research in the field of democratic modern society may be interpreted in different forms. It highlights those underlying forces and processes through which political power is marshalled and applied in organized societies, preferably in democracies. A pluralistic society, with a democratic order, recognizes the existence of pressure group and ensures widest possible participation to the extent of making them the principal avenues of activity out of the official administration. There is a fact remains in every society, whether democratic or totalitarian, that pressure groups seek to influence public policy in a desired direction without being ready to accept the responsibility of public office as well as by declining to hold direct responsibility for ruling the country.

In this present day socio-economic and political conditions of Manipur, the role of the voluntary organizations or associations as a pressure group is very important. The increasing discontent of the people, repeated failure of crops, the steep devaluation of the rupee, pressure from foreign governments, mounting bribery and corruption, the havoc created by castieism, linguism and regionalism etc. put democracy on a trial in India. In an underdeveloped society like Manipur, where there is a big question on the functional process of democracy and its effectiveness, the immediate needs is of a free society of free man– which is a basic necessity of a functional and effective democracy. Really it is a big hurdle, a fierce and dangerous battle which can only be fought with the culture of peace.

When the people are not satisfied with the decision and policies of the government, which is unsuitable to the public, they formally complain to the government.If the government does not consider or take into account the complaint, then the affected persons along with others can protest or even call strike against the government. Thus the people can curb the wrongful activities of the government. Protest and strikes may in course of time develop into a form of political movement with the help of the mass media. The degree of political participation of the people increased in the socio-political movement through the activities of pressure group.

Now-a-days the socio-economic and political situation of Manipur is characterized by a great sense of resentment with different demands and pressures. The various prevailing problems made the people of Manipur, especially youth and women more acquainted with socio-economic and political conditions of the society. These problems are sometimes natural and most of the time a creation of man and circumstances which hampered the activities of the government in a big way but Manipur an already under-developed part of North East India needs a government whose activities are quick, clear and effective. For avoiding such situations the role of the civil society is very much important. Due to the gap between the input and output, as well as problems in the feedback in the political system social dissatisfaction bring the people together to form groups and perform the function of pressure groups. When these groups became a formal organization, it is very difficult for the government not to heed their pressure. As a result, different associations and organizations mushroom up in the length and breadth of Manipur and giving pressure to the government according to the time and need of the society. It is right time to study about the role of pressure groups in the development of a society through a democratic process. And again it is also necessary to study about the formation, activities, function, importance etc. of the civil society organizations, especially women in the present social context.

Review of the Literature

The study of pressure group is beset with the task of precise nomenclature and other problems of a procedural and substantive character. All groups are not the same, though they are distinguished as such, e.g. some represent vested interests or interest of a particular social or economic group having some sort of objective characteristics common to each other, others represent and safeguard the interest of a particular point, regardless of their objective characteristics. Then, these groups are of different types— self seeking and altruistic from the viewpoint of purpose, ephemeral and long term keeping in view the point of tenure, and with formal or informal bureaucratic organizations taking in view the fact of power position. Likewise, these groups are different from each other as regards their concentration of efforts either on the legislative bodies or on the voters as a whole. Differences are also visible when we examine the functional impact of pressure politics upon a particular policy and, that is why, some groups frequently achieve their goals while others to do so. On the whole, pressure groups have a very important role in a modern political system where the state is irrevocably wedded to the ideals of representative democracy and social welfare. The term pressure group has come into used to signify and aggregate, organized or unorganized group which applies pressure tactics. It is defined as "any combination of persons, bound together by shared goals and attitudes, who attempt to obtain decisions favourable to their preferred values by all means at their disposal but specially by gaining access to the governmental process." A.de. Grazia in his book. "The Elements of Political Science" defines pressure groups simply as any organized social group that seeks to influence the behaviour or political officers without seeking formal control of the government. H. Zeigler in his book "Interest Groups in American Society" defined a pressure group as "an organized aggregate which seeks to influence the context of governmental decisions without attempting to place its members in formal governmental capacities."[4] People used pressure group as synonymous with interest group. But the scope of pressure group is larger than that of interest group. Pressure group is employed to describe any collection of persons through political action to influence public policy common objectives, who seek their realization through political action to influence public policy. Still more simply, an interest group is any that wants something from government. Regarding this McIver stated that, "When a number of men united for the defence, maintenance or enhancement of any more or less enduring position or advantage which they possess alike in common, the term 'interest' is applied both to the group so united and the causes which unites them. In the sense, the term is most frequently used in the plural, implying either that various similar groups or advantages combine to form a coherent complex, as in the term vested interests or that the uniting interest is maintained against an opposing one, as in the expressions conflict of interest or balance of interest. Interests so understood usually have an economic-political character."[5] With reference to the activities of pressure group in developed countries, Henry A. Turner stated that, "By definition pressure groups are non-partisan organizations which attempt to influence some phase of public policy. They do not themselves draft party programmes or nominate candidates for public office. Pressure associations do, however, appear before the resolution committees of the political parties to urge the endorsement of their programme as planks in the party platforms. They often attempt to secure the endorsement of both major parties and thus remove their programme from the arena of partisan controversy. Many groups are also active in the nomination and election of party members to public offices."[6] For having a clear knowledge of pressure group activities it is necessary to review the existence and articulation of pressure groups in various countries of the world which are having different types of political system. First, we can take up the case of a country having Presidential system of government like the United States, where the legislature and executive are separated from each other, for this reason, the pressure groups have to exercise their influence upon two organs of the government separately. They have their eyes fixed mostly on the President, who is the virtual ruler of the country and when they fear some frustrations, they apply their potential articulations through the legislative bodies with the result that there is pressure and cross-pressure to bear upon the government.[7] Second, the same degree of freedom of action for the interplay of pressure group is not allowed in a parliamentary system of the British model where political parties on the basis of their numerical strength form either the Government or the Opposition and run their organization on the basis of strict discipline. Besides, the party commanding majority in the popular chamber forms the government and thereby implements its policy and programme as given in the party manifesto or announced at the platform.[8] Third, the multi-party system of government in France with traditions of violent revolution is responsible for making the position of institutional and anomic groups more important than that is obtaining in Britain; and in India, also there are pressure groups but these pale into insignificance when compared to their American counterparts. Some of the groups and lobbies are sympathetic towards certain parties and interests. The Forum of Free Enterprise and the American Lobby in India which are strongly in favour of private enterprise go hand in hand with the Swatantra Party.[9] In France the Communist Party has its groups in the trade Union organizations and certain institutional groups (like the Catholic Church) have their colonies in the political parties and pressure groups interpenetrate each other.[10] Fourth, a dominant non-authoritarian party systems are usually to be found where nationalist movements have been instrumental in attaining emancipation in a totalitarian model. Exceptionally a reference should be made to the developing societies where pressure groups do exist though in a rudimentary and poorly organized form. The techniques they often adopt are of a very crude type. When a serious crisis comes, the military supervenes to finish the obtaining order and establish its dictatorship by virtue of its coherent organization, similarly of outlook and the capacity to organize the coup. In such a society other interest may be powerless to move because of their lack of organization and discipline; they will have to come to terms with the colonels, but will retain some strength since the colonels cannot run state without at least some co-operation from them.[11]

So, simply pressure group signifies the existence of a group life. It is an attempt not of particular individual or a group attempt, a concerted effort. This group may be an elite or teacher or student or youth or like other categories. The most common denominator for all interest articulation is the sharing of attitude. Beyond their individual peculiarities men are conditioned by their group loyalties. The common motivations of different sections or classes are in fact the building blocks of the group shaped by the interaction within the group, the experiences of its members etc. Pressure groups cannot operate without formal organizations, without which an average citizen is an innocent by standard and also a bewildered one. Organization represents concentrated power which can exercise a dominating influence in the political process. In a real sense the pressure groups are not law making agencies at the same time they attempt to help the legislature to pass laws in their favour. It implies external inducement to control the behaviour of the legislators.

Dr. Karam Manimohan Sing, in his book 'Nupilal', clearly mentioned about the importance of movement of the masses against the ruling authority when they were the suppressed and forbidden class in their own society. In the society where rights and equality were senseless words printed in the books; and the British and their nominated Rulers in many of the Native states of India were the strong and the mighty people, they were the Paramount Hunters and the people the Hunted. In such situations mass movements or civil war had to occur. It was very natural and nobody could suppress it before it broke out. The agitation was the hopeless resort for the poor people to ventilate their old desires and genuine grievances but with a far hope of attaining a culturally and socially higher and more acceptable activity. The disturbances known as the Nupilal, which took place in Imphal during the winter of 1939, brought to a head the question of introducing reforms into the Manipur state as November 1938, when the Maharaja received a petition signed by 356 members of the public asking for the setting up of a Legislative Council. Next year in November 1939, Irabot as the President of the Nikhil Manipur Mahasabha again submitted an outline of the Legislature to His Highness the Maharaja for necessary actions so that the legitimate rights of the people may be secured and the grievances redressed.[12]

Methodology

Controlled experiment in social science research is a difficult one, but fruitful observation is feasible as mentioned by Bryce and A.L. Lowell. So, observation method is used by the author for writing this book. Data are gathered, analyzed and classified after coming in contact with and observing and studying the activities of different women organizations related and involved with them at a close range. This vollume work is not depending on hearsay or second hand information only. The author visited directly to the areas of pressure group's performed their activities and make careful observation about all happenings and prepared notes of what is happenings with minute details. For achieving a thorough objective and scientific generalization, I seek interviews and have recorded voices and photographs of the events. And, again, for further information, I collect questionnaire reports from the related persons. So both the types of observations :

(1) Participant observation

(2) Non-participant observation

are employed for collection of primary data. Observation is carried out with the help of the eye, and the purpose and aim of observation is to discover significant mutual relations between spontaneously occurring events and thereby pinpoint significant facts of a situation. It is quite plain from these remarks that observation is not random perception, but in the sense of a deliberate effort to pinpoint significant facts, that observation is considered to be a scientific method. Here the definition of Mrs. P.V. Young is quite applicable, "Observation is a systematic and deliberate study, through the eye of spontaneous occurrences at the time they occur. The purpose of observation is to perceive the nature and extent of significant interrelated elements within complex social phenomena, culture, pattern, or human conduct."[13]

All the three prerequisite conditions of observation mentioned by B.N. Ghosh in his book, Scientific and Social Research, i.e. intellectual, physical and moral[14]are strictly followed. The reason and explanation of phenomenon came from intellectual faculty and introspection. Perfect physical capability and sound sense organs are used for proper observation in all the field visits and events from time to time. The required moral conditions related to unbiasedness and impartiality is strictly kept in mind as the research work is covering all the delicate issues of different communities. Subjective inclination, conservatism, superstitions, habits etc. are entirely given up while making observations. There is no pre-conceived notion or bias about that which is being observed for finding out the truth.

Objectives

The main objectives of the publication of this book are as follows—

1. To discuss about the growth and relevance of women organization in the society, especially in Manipur.
2. To analyze the value of women organization in a democratic system of government.
3. To discuss about the problems faced by the people due to the failure of the application of the democratic norms.
4. To study about the relationship between the women organizations and other pressure groups.
5. To study the action and reaction of women organization as a pressure group in the democratic process of Manipur.
6. To find out the necessary consequential steps for strengthening democratic values with the proper activities of the women organization as a pressure group.

Women Organisations and Pressure Groups in Manipur

Women play a very important role in the social life of Manipur. In the developmental activities the involvement of women should be prerequisite for proper and speedy development. A long lasting peace cannot be established without the participation of women and girls and the inclusion of gender perspectives in the formal and informal peace processes.Women have long been active in lobbying and organizing for peace and disarmament. Grassroots women's groups have organized across party and ethnic lines, advocating for peace and carrying out reconciliation efforts. They have called for the elimination of weapons of mass destruction, campaigned against small arms, participated in weapon collection programmes, disseminated information on landmines etc. Mothers have organized to learn the fate of their "disappeared" children, or to prevent them from being conscripted or sent to war or to any illegal activities or even any type of work that is not felt by their age. Women, generally in a developing country like India and particularly in an underdeveloped, remote, boarder state like Manipur, take a great role in the process for the development of the society, by resolving almost all the conflicting situations, which are happening from time to time. For Manipur without them the progress and development of the society is impossible. Theoretically, women in North East India, and especially in Manipur, enjoy a high social status because their societies are egalitarian. There is no restriction on women's movements, food habits, attire, widow remarriage etc. In Manipur, cultural and social factors not operate vigorously and exclusively in favour of any sex. There is hardly any dowry problem, hardly any problem of sex preference, etc. Historical evidences can be traced in the state where females took major roles in the state, regional and national issues. Mention may be made of the two different famous women's movements of Manipur-Nupilal of 1904; and Nupilal of 1939, where Manipuri women resisted the Imperial to denigrate the Manipuri's by the Political Agent of British Government, the then Maharaja and Marwari Monopolists etc. The living example that Manipur society is not a female discriminating society is the existence of "Nupi Keithel" (a market where vendors are exclusively run by women) at the heart of Imphal, the capital city of Manipur.[15] Although the status of women is said to be higher but men in their own societies do not treat the women as their equal. The customary laws of the various tribes in this region are in favour of man who continues to superiority *vis-à-vis* women in their respective societies. Except the Khasis of Meghalaya which matrilineal system, other tribal communities of North East India have Patriarchal family structure. Women in the patriarchal families usually do not enjoy equal status with their husband or male members in their families. Women may be said to enjoy more freedom in their families and social activities. But when we talk of gender equality, women are dominated by their family or clans. Major decisions in their families are taken by their husbands and other male members of the family. The economy of the states in North East India is mainly based on agriculture. The type of agriculture in the states of North East region; particularly in tribal areas is jhum or shifting cultivation. This type of cultivation is associated with high female work participation. It is also called female farming system, characterized by few wage labourers and large female participation. Women have performed a clear, significant and approved role in the field of production and marketing. Women of the country, India, are fully protected by laws and they are better placed than women in the Western countries. It means, both men and women are equal in law and any discrimination on the basis of sex alone is illegal and unlawful in India. In the West there is social equality, denied voting rights, they were not treated even as citizens in the West in the case of election. It is their fight for legal equality and citizenship that prompted the formation of feminism in the West. But there in India, the women have legal equality, and legal rights along with men. There is no discrimination on the basis of sex alone. But social equality is not there. Because India's social system and the reason for this social system is due to historical circumstances. Historical circumstances cannot be changed, society can be changed, everybody says. But those who preached social change forgot the fact that these preachers themselves should change first, as unless individuals themselves are not changed, the society which is constituted by individuals cannot be changed. Changed in social system is not that much easy.[16] Law itself cannot change society wholly. Yet unfortunately, the various laws of the countries, provisions of the U.N., the various Women's Commissions and Human Rights Commission staffed by the elite groups of the society have been unable to do anything for the protection and upliftment of the suffering and exploited poor women section.

The number of crimes against women is increasing day-by-day. Maximum headlines of the daily papers and journals are focusing on women issues and crimes. Immoral activities, sex mafia, drug menace, violence, and communal friction cases in the courts are the common issues. Partially of the police in investigation and manipulating crucial evidence at the instigation of politicians and other vested interests also contributed for the increase. Women and girls are not only victims in armed conflict, they are also active agents, and even they become wife conditionally and bear children of those armed groups. This situation was exhibited on the first day of the operation 'Summer Storm' at Loktak of Bisnnupur District in Manipur, during the second weak of April 2009. They may choose to participate in the conflict or to provide non-military support; or they may be manipulated or forced into various roles. Women and girls may be forced into sexual slavery or coerced to work as domestic servants for fighting groups. Many women organize for conflict resolution, peacemaking and disarmament. They are involved in rebuilding the social, cultural, economic and political fabric of their societies. It appears that Indian society has been almost criminalized and crimes have been increased considerably. No statistic will reveal the whole truth. The motive behind all these crimes is greed for money, position, and for luxuries of life, sexual urge, personal hatred, enmity and envy. But even where women have been involved in informal peace processes, they are normally pushed into the background when formal peace process begins.

Often women themselves do not recognize their activities as part of peace building efforts, because these are in areas for which women are already responsible, such an ensuring the safety of themselves and their families and accessing and providing social services. Because women lack formal political platforms, they often draw credibility and strength from a wider social base and promote their agenda at the grassroots level. As a result, women's contributions tend to be undervalued and not readily incorporated or sought by many practitioners of peace building.

Peace processes themselves have been described as including informal activities and formal activities. Informal activities include peace marches, intergroup dialogue, and the promotion of inter-cultural tolerance and understanding. As an informal peace process of Assam Rifles, they organized cultural programmes with the local people, involved in the local programme, held interaction with the women groups etc. During February-March 2009, Assame Rifles arranged a national tour programme of the Meira Paibis. Before and after the programme they have interacted with the women groups. Formal activities generally involve a range of UN entities, regional/national/local institutions, and grassroots organizations. Formal activities are conducted by political leaders, the military, international and regional/sub-regional institutions, and a variety of governmental and non-governmental organizations.[17] A number of peace-keeping operations have taken steps to address violence against women and girls and trafficking. Activities include public awareness campaigns, training of the local police, supporting local organizations and developing special mechanisms within local low enforcement structures. Peace-keeping missions in Bosnia and Herzegovina, Kosovo and East Timor have worked to promote gender balance in the local police force and trained new or restructured police forces on domestic violence and trafficking in women and girls. The missions in Kosovo and East Timor also supported the increased participation of women in the governmental and administrative structures through training and capacity building. Peace-keeping missions can benefit from contact with civil society, including women's organizations and networks, to understand the specific impact of armed conflict and the effects of peace-keeping operations on women and girls.

While women's involvement in informal activities is well documented, they are seldom included in formal activities, reflecting the fact that they are usually not represented among decision makers and military leaders. This should be cause for concern since issues affecting women will not be expressed if women are not consulted by fact finding missions or involved in peace negotiations: "political structures, economic institutions and security sectors negotiated in peace talks will not facilitate greater equality between women and men if gender dimensions are not considered in these discussions".

Women, being perceived as 'not political', are more able to access information and pressure authorities to provide services to minimize the impact of conflict on the civilian population. They are also able to occupy spaces to develop community level initiatives for peace across ethnic and national identities. On the other hand, women as symbols of community and/or ethnic identity may become the targets of extensive sexual violence. In this case, the public space becomes similar to the private space of the home in which women often experience daily violence.

Armed conflict and its aftermath affect women's lives in ways that differ from the impact on men. In most conflicts, the traditional division of civilian space—private as women's space and public as men's space—collapses. Men in communities under attack tend to abandon public spaces to avoid being conscripted, attack, or taken hostage. In this vacuum, women increasingly become the ones to manouver through existing institutions (from market to government departments) and to provide for family welfare and security, including taking on roles traditionally assigned to men.

Women experience inequality in power relative to men from the household level to the national level where they are universally underrepresented in legislative bodies, organs of government and local political structures. Women belonging to poor, lower class category experience more problems than the women of rich and higher class families. Women, especially those with low incomes, tend to have less control over their time. These factors are closely linked to their nutritional status, the quality of care they receive and the nutritional status of their children. The health consequences for women and girls during conflict are enormous. Women and girls are highly vulnerable, due to their sexual and reproductive roles. Gender discrimination can lead to inequitable distribution of food to women and girls, causing malnutrition and other health problems. Women's daily tasks as providers and caregivers become increasingly difficult and dangerous, especially as public services and household goods become less and less available. Armed conflict forces women to take on more responsibilities for family security and livelihoods. But lack of land and property rights constrains their efforts. Women and girls take on new or non-traditional occupations. Forced out of the formal sector and with increasing competition in the informal sector, they may be pushed into dangerous illegal activities. Experiencing or witnessing death, separation, rape, torture, destruction, loss of livelihood and material deprivation can cause severe mental and social stress. Armed conflict also changes social structures and relations. Women as well as men are victims of detention and 'disappearance'. The 'disappearance' of male relatives particularly affects women in societies where their status is directly linked to their relationships with men. Women are traumatized and cannot find closer as long as they still hope for the return of their relatives.

Gender is one of the world's strongest markers for disadvantage. This is specially the case in South Asia. The large number of missing women in the region bears testimony to the scale of the problem. Disadvantage starts at birth. In India, the death rate for children of ages 1-5 is 15 per cent higher for girls than boys. Expressed differently 1,30,000 young lives are lost every year because of the disadvantage associated with being born with two x chromosomes (HDR 2005). The Constitution of India guarantees equal rights for women with men and equal treatment before law. The pertinent question is how these can, need of social bonding, harmony and equity, be fulfilled. Through new awakening, new ideas, actions, movements, persuasive and consciousness raise conversation, legislation and policy planning no doubt, which may be socio-politically engineered. In most cases, all these are expressed in the ethic of justice which stressed the importance of the dignity of the individual and personal liberty. If the appalling condition of women caused by long entrenched inequity of the sexes is to be eradicated, men and women must jointly wage a war against a system—a system of power relationship by which women are subordinated.

To strive for equality with men (modernity) is also disastrous for the women in the contemporary world in several ways. For women who is more active, clever and successful with high status, the mounting fear is that she may be judged by men as less sexually attractive, loss of a real woman and definitely more threatening than other woman. There is a kind of gender power reflected in tactics of impression management both in real and imaginary world. Several of them would be taboo for women in comparison with men. Women are private and men are public. The role of women in the family is becoming more and more important. Women are seen as inseparable from the family, and most functions assigned to the family are allocated to women within it. Women are usually the careers, the nurturers, the educators, the source of stability, and increasingly they are major cash contributors. For the most past, women meet their responsibilities to their children, their men and older or infirm relatives with generosity, self-sacrifice and unstinting labour. The family affects every aspect of women's lives their socialization and education, their sexuality, the way in which they are expected to behave as women, wives, mothers and cares. The outcomes of the twenty-four hour multitasking of women are not counted.

The family places immense obligations on women's shoulders and shapes their places and role in the community and in local, national and international affairs.

A major face of gender discrimination is the unequal distribution of property rights between men and women. In developing countries, women's rights of ownership over economic assets and legal structures that support these are weak. In most conditions, women's property rights over land are either insecure or virtually non-existent. Retention of such rights is also poor, in the absence of adequate statutory protection. Insecurity in women's property rights over primary resources is the principal issue of gender inequalities within agrarian households. Perpetuation of unequal property structures stems from the need for patriarchal institutions to exercise power over land as a productive resource and as a generator of wealth. Most literature on property rights, however, leaves the gender characteristics of property rights undefined, thus failing to recognize the inter-household consequences of rights inequalities on the distribution of rights and responsibilities within and without the household.

While writing on the subjection of women in early industrial societies, J.S. Mill had anticipated some of the current feminist arguments while stating that political equality of women would be the combined outcome of personal freedom from patriarchal control as well as equal educational and economic opportunities, equal political rights and equal property rights. On such egalitarian principles, liberal feminist theories have thus advocated gender parity between men and women. Radical feminist theories however disagree with the egalitarian conceptualization of gender justice, on the ground that it merely focuses on surface economic issues, leaving the structural inequalities that affect women untouched.

Another important discourse informing current perceptions about gender roles and rights has arisen within development economics. Several gender adaptations have consequently been made to development practice. Women are now being seen as autonomous economic agents who need to be independently reached by gender equity and poverty alleviation programmes that leverage their household functions in order to create an economic and social security net around rural families and simultaneously improve their participation in economic activities by raising their command over productive resources. Among the primary constituents of women's autonomy, are women's property rights.

While it has been argued that the obliteration of gender inequalities within households and societies through the realization of private property rights by women would also eliminate many insecurities relating to the livelihood and well-being of women, it is nevertheless also necessary for women to secure gender based usufructuary rights that are often crucial to their survival as productive agents in subsistence economies. Gender disparities within common property rights are known to have significantly affected the outcomes of policies for natural resource management in terms of efficiency, environmental sustainability, equity and empowerment of resource users. Other than customary land inheritance and the right to hold personal property in other forms, the traditional property rights held by women have mainly comprised usufruct rights on properties belonging collectively to the family or community. Such usufruct rights have also been vital to the performance of paid and unpaid women's work, they relate closely to the social positioning and status of women in rural communities

In India, for centuries, women have been pushed aside from the path of development in the name of custom, tradition and religion. As a result, they have been denied opportunities for social, economic and political development. This has driven them to lower status in the society. Eradication of poverty was one of the priorities of India's national reconstruction. "Garibi Hatao" (remove poverty) was in the air for some time. But that slogan failed as it was more of a political tone than a whole-hearted, participatory programme sponsored by the common men and women in the country. Out of 850 million people about 700 million live in the villages. Half of these are women and a sizeable portion of children, old and invalid persons who are dependent on the earning members of the family. These rural folks are still in the grip of illiteracy, ignorance and superstitions. The rate of illiterate women in Manipur is 4,14,341 out of total 11,31,944 female population according to 2001 census. Several factors are responsible for the widespread illiteracy of women in some states of North East India. Looking after the younger brothers and sisters at home, household works, bringing water and firewood from outside, working in other's houses, working in the fields etc. to earn livelihood are considered to be the main duties of the girls and women in rural and hill areas. Drop-out rate in most of the hill areas in North East India is also very high. It is not a matter of discrimination against girls but mainly due to economic factors, non-availability of school, colleges etc. in nearby areas are also seemed to be important factors. Even though agriculture and cattle breeding, small scale industries, craft and other handicrafts are the main openings for employments for rural population, these do not generate enough income to meet the subsistence of these people. Employment is only for a few while under-employment and non-employment rules the rostrum. In majority of village families it is the women who are the breadwinners and they maintain the family while the majority of men idle away their time by playing dices, enjoying *hukka* and killed the time.[17] Poverty and unemployment have the worst effect on women leading to the phenomenon of feminization of poverty. Poverty is a part of our social culture from time immemorial. It emanates from the philosophy of self-denial. It is customary in Indian families to serve best part of the food to the male members of the family, especially the earning members of the family so that they maintain their health for hard work. The balance is distributed to the children and the old. If anything is left in the earthen pot, then the women in the family share it.[18] This, of course, has been changed now thanks to the improvement made by the various Five Year Plans and other schemes sponsored by Government and voluntary organizations, such as banks, cooperative societies etc. Yet it is not possible to eradicate poverty from our land completely in spite of our earnest effort. Much has yet to be done and here the women's organizations and autonomous groups can purposefully play their role. In fact, women's organizations and research wings have done valuable studies on the reason for persisting poverty in Indian rural areas.[19] The march of Indian women from orthodoxy to equality is quite fascinating and spontaneous. General education and innumerable enactments of British Indian Government facilitated a fresh air of freedom to Indian women. The Indian women attempted to fly out of the cage like free birds, and soar in the western horizon of independence and equality. British India is a witness to testify that from the very enactment of prohibiting *Sati,* infanticide and early marriage of the girl child to the present day law of equal share of the parental property to both the son and the daughter is an apparent example of road to freedom for the Indian women. Even now highlighting female rights and priorities are containing in independent India by democratic enactment and procedures and a stage has come that Indian women has reached to the level of Indian men in all aspects of life in this country. To further improve their position and status, many commissions and projects have been launched in the past fifty eight years. The latest being National Women Commission, they have been given equal rights with men as per Constitution and as per every law of the country[20]. Women can do many a thing if they are united. After all it is well said, union is strength. The unity of women can help very much to reduce their hardships. Every nation has its own problems. Yet the women's forum will accelerate welfare measures among women in the respective countries. Women's union in villages, panchayats, taluks, districts and state levels can handle women's problems very successfully.[21] Women's unions can top and utilize the funds allotted by governments, quasi-governments and charitable organizations and private parties interested decide the mode of action to be taken by them in that particular area. When the state is full of such "active women's union" all women's problems will get due attention and that can be solved early by concerned authorities. The local women's union can also organize agitation against all the problems like environmental problems, e.g. Narmada Bachao Andolan (Save Narmada Movement) of Medha Patker. Human rights issues, e.g., Remove Armed Forces Special Power Act, 1958 from Manipur of Sharmila Chanu. They can even unleash agitation against liquor shops, ration shop manipulation and black-marketing and price rise etc. Such concrete and practical works on the women's part will go a long way to relieve the poor and downtrodden women in the country. Women's peace movements often focus on shared experiences and produce solidarity across lines of division, which make it hard to cast the enemy as 'the other'. The concerns these groups have about their children and other family members give them a social legitimacy and a linkage with women from different sides of the conflict. As a result, women have sometimes fewer difficulties than men in expressing concerns about a conflict.

The greatest obstacles to women's unity and solidarity in India are religious, caste and language. While these were the part and parcel of Indian culture and civilization, spurious and superfluous customs and conventions silently crept into the society in course of time. While what is best is to be retained the rest has to be discarded. Resurrecting the past will not serve us in future. At the same time human values and virtues must be nourished and nurtured and made the part of life for both man and woman. As women comprise nearly half of the total population of the country this denial has contributed in no small measures to India's continuing development.

In India, different writings, epics, novels etc. reveal that women have been given very high status. But it is necessary to examine whether the women are giving the value of the real position or not, or in what way they are interpreting. In the Ramayana, Ram though an Avatar of Vishnu was helpless in killing the demon Ravana. Ram had to worship goddess Durga in order to obtain supernatural power. Ultimately he did that and was able to kill the demon. Instances are legion where feminine power has been rated very high, nay, even superior to masculine power. Further Ram could not perform any religious function in the absence of Sita; therefore, he would keep a statue of Sita made of gold by his side and would perform the religious rites. Even the earth has been visualized as the mother for it is this mother earth which gives us shelter in her lap at the time of birth and death. Even the rivers like Ganges, Yamuna and Saraswati have been elevated to the status of mother. Insult, injury or any kind of humiliation to mother has been cursed as Matri Haran Dosa (unpardonable sin against womenfolk by men). All these instances and scriptural testimonies show that at least in the textual and ideational level Indian women were accorded very high position. Even in some oral traditions of a section of Nagas the highest Being is a female called 'emonopfii' or 'ukepenopfii'. In the Hindu oral tradition it is said that a house where women are respected Gods are pleased there. This theme has been vividly and colourfully described in a 15th century literary work by Balaram Das in *Laxmi Purana*. Lord Jagannath who is known to be an Avatar of Vishnu along with his elder brother Balaram had to suffer from abject poverty and humiliation because he disrespected his wife Laxmi (the Goddess of wealth). Only when Laxmi was propitiated Jagannath and Balaram got back their lost glory and status.[22] Now it is quite clear that women were being used by their male counterparts to serve/fulfil their own vested interersts or purposes. In a real sense, women are givers and males are receivers. Women are exploited and males are exploiters.

The emergence of the rudiments of a women's movement in India can be seen in the formation of and growth of women's association over a period of 50 years, from roughly 1880 to 1930. The rudiments were the aggregate of local, provincial and national associations oriented towards improving the position of women and aiding national development.

Women play a very important role in the social life of Manipur. A study of social life and social change of Manipur will be uncompleted without a study on women. Women participate in multifarious activities of socio-economic and political matters. Women who are facing a number of problems in connection with the socio-economic and political condition form different organizations. The main concern of these organizations are not only women's issues, but raised all other social issues such as discrimination of the minorities, negligence to culture, language, marginalization due to the developmental process leading to displacement, loss of work, loss of identity and impoverishment in a massive scale, violation of human rights etc. social movements are an effort to change institutions and practices. They are usually for the purpose of furthering the rights of one or more groups within a system either through reform or more radical changes. Social movements labour to alter fundamentally existing social relationship and institutional structures.[23] The area of work covered by the activities of women's group and network is not confining to a limited area of state and national level. Internationally, women's groups and networks have begun to work at regional and sub-regional levels. For example, the African Women's Committee on Peace and Development, launched in 1999, focuses on promoting conflict resolution in a number of African countries. The Mano River Women's Peace Network brings together women from Guinia, Liberia and Sierra Leone.[24] Consultations with women's groups and networks can provide insights on conflict situations. Understanding gender norms and customs in a society may provide important imformations for early warning. But international organizations have not always recognized and utilized women's knowledge, experience and informal involvement in peace processes. Assessment missions focus almost exclusively on political parties and other formal political actors. The then UN Secretary General, Kofi Anan made an action propose during the formation of Security Council Resolution 1325 (2000).[25]

1. Integrate gender perspectives into the terms of reference of Security Council visits and missions to countries and regions in conflicts; request briefings on the situation of women and girls in conflicts; include gender specialists wherever possible; and ensure consultation with women's groups and networks.
2. Ensure that all peace accords address the consequences of the impact of armed conflict on women and girls, their contributions to the peace process and their needs and priorities in the aftermath of a conflict.
3. Ensure full involvement of women in negotiations of peace agreement at national and international levels, including through provision of training for women and women's organizations on formal peace processes.

In Manipur, the role of women in social movements can be traced back to the Pre British period when Manipur was under monarchical system, when the policies and activities of the king affected the social norms, structure etc., of the society, women in an organized form represented before the king and expressed their viewpoints. In most of these cases the king very often changed the policies as requested by the society. Raja Paikhomba (1666-1697), could not appoint Ingallei as Rani because people of Manipur refused to accept her as their Rani. The voices of the masses came so to think that Maharani was not merely the wife of the King but also the queen cf the people and, therefore, acceptable to them. Above all she must be an example to them. The Maharani should be a model woman so that women in the kingdom might copy her.[26]

Women's social movement emerged in a more organized manner with a creative ideology from the early part of the 20th century. Women's movement in Manipur is norm oriented type and connected with reformations. Social movements came into being as a reaction to the discontent, dissatisfaction and contradiction in the then society of Manipur.

The first Nupilal (women's movement) of 1904 was a reaction to the contemporary social problems. The immediate cause of the movement was the revival of Lallup. The Political Agent ordered the villagers to collect bamboos, thatch, reeds and other materials for the construction of the Bangalow. Again, all the people of Imphal (at least one male member of the family) were ordered to extract teak wood from Kabow for the construction of the House of the Assistant Superintendent which the people protested and assembled at Bazar. The Meitei women took main part in the protest. From the side of the government all sorts of means were used for controlling the movement, using army, lathi charged, even more than five persons were not allowed to assemble etc. But the women did not stop their movement; they disobeyed the orders, entered into the residence of the Political Agent and Superintendent. They were injured but their relentless activities were unable to control by the British

Officers. So the system of Lallup was stopped and peace restored in the country.

Another important and remarkable women's movement during the British period was the movement of 1939, i.e. Second Nupilal. The immediate cause for the outburst of the women's movement of 1939 was the economic important arising out of the scarcity of rice in Manipur. The rice export was exclusively controlled by the Marwari traders during that time. They exported rice to other parts of British India. The Marwari traders who were permanently settled in Manipur held the top position in the economic structure of Manipur. They had the monopoly of purchasing of rice and paddy from the cultivators and local traders. As a result, the local people suffered a lot. The nature of the movement was quite democratic, but the authority tried to control the movement by using forces. The women were not ready to stop but became more serious which leads to the closer of rice mills by the concerned authority. This was a clear example of the spirit of women's movement touching the economic aspect of the society before independence, even though the whole responsibility of the family was in the hands of the male head of the family as a patriarchal society.

Every sovereign state and its subdivisions has at its disposal an armory of measures to preserve, maintain, and restore law and order and to protect the lives and property of its citizens in times of unrest when there is a high likelihood of violence or when violence erupts against the government itself or between large segments of the population. Among such measures are the imposition of martial laws, restrictions on the rights of *habeas corpus*, declaration of emergency, that provide the government with extraordinary powers, and the imposition of curfew.[27] When the Britishers left Manipur and she became a part of the Indian Union in 1949, she was hoping of protection internally and externally. The earlier hopes of the people of Manipur were shattered as in the name of protection and maintenance of law and order, their basic rights have been robbed constantly. The people of that time believe for a developed and welfare society under the different constitutional provisions. But in the name of the maintenance of law and order of the state, different military forces arrived in the state along with different Acts and Bills, which hampered the rights of the people, even including all human rights. The role of women in the civil society of North East India generally, and Manipur especially has a significant record. Women organizations have come forward for peace in Manipur and organize resistance against police excesses, bad governance, shortage of basic needs etc.

By the late 1970s and with the beginning of 1980s the entire state of Manipur was under heavy combing operation by the army in order to flush out the extremists. During the operation a number of innocent people suffered a lot, including women. During that time women, who were directly affected by actions of the Police and Paramilitary forces, along with other local women started to guard their family members. This movement of women came to be known as Meira Paibi movement. If there are any serious problems which are likely to affect peaceful social atmosphere of the locality, it is made compulsory for every house to join this movement, ever since the women in different parts of the state have been organizing themselves against the activities of armed personals, and other related issues. In different occasions, women in different sections gathered in front of the Chief Minister's or Governor's Bangalow and soughed anti- combing slogan or excesses of armed personals, which are followed by big demonstrations, hartals, bands etc. This has some amount of desire effect.

While the women are facing a number of problems in connection with the socio-economic and political development of the country, the existing government do not protect even the prestige of the women and the society altogether. As a recent trend, suicide of the newly married women, killing of innocent people, kidnapping etc., are becoming the common problems of Manipur. In the armed conflict situations, many Manipuri's have lost their lives. In such situations the weaker and backwards are the worst sufferers. In case of Manipur also women and rural backward people are the worst sufferers. Women have fallen victims to the carnal desires of the armed personnels, both, state and non-state forces. Many rape cases by the army goes unreported due to the fear of social stigma and the futility of taking up embarrassing death battle against the might of the Army Personnels in the name of the maintenance of law and order in the State is becoming unbearable to the women. So some women, under the leadership of All Manipur Social Reformer and Development Samaj protested against the Assam Rifles in a nude position against the custodial rape and killing of Thangjam Manorama, on 11 July 2004 at Bamon Kampu in Imphal East District of Manipur. They have done this by thinking that upon their bodies, women carry the honours of their community. The rape and abduction of women constitute dishonouring of the male members of the community and of the community as a whole. In many societies women are also seen as more traditional, conservative, and religious than their men and thereby as upholders of the fundamental values of the community.[28] Women are simultaneously critical and incidental. Through women, men multiply their race, increase their members. They are, in this way critical. But they are also incidental. They may be captured and put to good use, unlike men of the other community, who represent a physical danger and, even when converted, are distrusted and not fully accepted.[29]

The pressure and movements of Manipuri women in all the conflict situations tend therefore to be treated with certain derision or simply set aside as irrelevant. To counteract this, many women movements became more aggressive, rude and more violent like radical who feel they must blow up everything to set things right. But it should not create any negative impression upon the mind of the general public.

Violence is a political issue and it is relevant to all, both men and women are victims of violence in Manipur. In the name of the maintenance of law and order, the different acts and bills are using by the authority. With these acts and bills a number of innocent people have lost their life. Different women voluntary organizations like the All Manipur Nupi Marup, All Manipur Social Reformer and Development Samaj, The Kuki Women Human Rights Network, Kuki Mother's Association etc. are involving in all such issues in Manipur and tried to protect the basic minimum rights of the people, i.e. the right to life. In different occasions like the killing of innocent people, raping of women and looting of the properties by the C.R.P.F at Patsoi, killing of innocent people at the volley ball ground of Heirangoithong, killing of 18 innocent people in June 2001 in connection with the extension of Indo-Naga Cease-fire in Manipur, killing of 11 persons by the security personnel from 26 February to 10 March 2004 from different places of Imphal, kidnapping and killing of the innocent persons like Manoj Kumar Sethi, Luiningla Elizabeth etc., these women groups launched different movements and the government also could not remain silent.

Manipur created a new history of women's movement when Irom Chanu Sharmila launched hunger strike since November 3, 2000 in protest against killing of ten civilians at Malom by the Assam Rifles personnel following a bomb attack by the underground outfits on the armed personnel on 2nd November 2000. Even she shifted her hunger strike base to New Delhi for six months (October 2006 to March 2007). The national leaders did not pay heed to her demand for removal of Armed Forces Special Power Act- 1958. Sharmila was frustrated and came back to Imphal on 4th March, 2007. Another reason for her return to Imphal was the promises made by almost all the political parties in Manipur during the assembly poll (2007) campaign to lobby for repeal of the Act. Shri O. Ibobi Singh, The Chief Minister of Manipur commented in front of the AICC leaders at New

Delhi during March in connection with Sharmila's protest, the Act had already been lifted from seven assembly segments of Imphal Municipal areas and the law and order situation in the state is permitting, the Act could be repealed from the entire state. But Sharmila is still continuing her hunger strike because the people of Imphal East and West are not only the worst sufferers but the remaining population are also sufferers.[30] In the name of maintenance of law and order in the State and for bringing welfare to the society, a number of draconian laws have been enforced in the State causing untold suffering of the masses.

Significance of the Study (Conclusion)

Now it is necessary to understand that women are taking a large role in the socio-economic and political movement of Manipur. But an extraordinary situation is that all the women's movements in some societies like, Manipuri Society, were not concerned with the women's issues which have mentioned by different feminists. Women organizations have contributed, in no small measures, to women's development and social development. The area of present study is only on a small border State of India, i.e., Manipur, but it will contribute to the understanding of the continuity and changes in connection with the formation of women's group and their movement in every part of the whole world. It will be very helpful in understanding about the role of women in the democratic set up.

NOTES

1. South Asia Human Rights Documentation Center, Introducing Human Rights, Oxford University Press, 2006, p. 86.
2. Gokhale, B. K., *A Study of Political Theory*, Himalaya Publishing House, p. 263
3. *Modern political analysis* p. 10.

4. Zeigler, H. *Interest group in American society,* Englewood Cliffs New Jersey, Prantice Hall 1964, p. 134.
5. McIver, R. M. *Encyclopedia of the Social Sciences,* Vol. 7-8, p. 144.
6. Turner A. Henry, *"How Pressure Groups Operates",* in *The Annals of the American Academy of Political and Social Sciences,* Philadelphia, Vol. 319, September 1958, p. 65.
7. Johari, J. C. *Comparative Politics,* Sterling Publishers Pvt Ltd, New Delhi, 1982 p. 386.
8. *Ibid.*
9. Gokhale, B. K. *A Study of Political Theory,* Himalaya Publishing House, p. 398.
10. Johari, J. C. *of. Cit.* p.388.
11. Miler, *The Nature of Politics,* Garald Duckworth and Co, London, 1962, p. 78.
12. Karam Manimohan Sing, *Nupilal,* K. Premlata Devi, Imphal, 2006. p. 264.
13. Young. P. V., *Scientific Social Survey and Research,* Prentice Hall Inc. 1962, p.154.
14. Ghosh. B. N, *Scientific and Social Research,* Sterling Publishers Pvt Ltd, New Delhi 1985. P. 55.
15. Aribam Brajakumar Sharma, *Influx of Migrant into Manipur,* Publication Committee, United Committee Manipur, 2005
16. Kunjakan, K. A., *Feminism and Indian Realities,* Mittal Publication, New Delhi. 2002, p.228
17. *Ibid.,* p.322.
18. Ibid., p. 323.
19. *Ibid.,* p.324.
20. *Ibid.,* pp. 373-74.
21. *Ibid.,* p. 403.
22. Mao Xevier P., *Empowerment of Women and the Concept of Development,* in Ray B. Dutta and Ray Asok Kumar, Ed. *Dynamics of Power Relations in Tribal Societies of North East India,* Om Publications, New Delhi,2006, p. 116
23. Raina, Vinod, *Social Movements in India,* Alternatives, 5 Jan 2004 at http.
24. *United Nations Security Council Resolution* 1325 (2000)
25. *Ibid.*
26. N. Ibobi Sing, *Manipur Administration 1709-1907,* N. Ibetombi Devi, Imphal 2003 p. 46.
27. Paul, R. Brass, *Violence Forms of Collective, Riot, Pogroms, and Genocide in Modern India,* Three Essays Collectives, 2005, p. 103.

28. *Ibid*. p.50.
29. *Ibid*. p. 52.
30. Th. Binarani Devi, "*Women's Movement in Conflict Situation in Manipur*", in Asok Kumar Ray and Satyabrata Chakraborty (ed), *Society, Politics and Development in North East India*, Concept Publishing Company Pvt. Ltd., New Delhi, 2008, p. 111.

2

Meaning and Role of Pressure Groups in a Democratic Society

Democracy is the social power relationship which embodied itself in a general form of the state in this present day societies. For the sake of convenient exposition, as also because the division corresponds broadly to the fact, democrats can be divided into those who seek other values, like equality, which have seemed to require democratic form to produce them. If we follow the meaning of these ideals from their origin, we shall find that quite different forms of government result from each. The ideal of liberal democracy is expressed in a variety of familiar phrases, such as "Just government is government by consent of the governed," or "self- government", and it implies, in the works of various authors, voluntary associations for unhindered establishment and operation of political parties, freedom of opinion, the subjection of government to popular control, the limitation of the sphere of government, and the universal possibilities of active participation in the process of government.[1] Thinkers like Kant, Herbert, Spencer etc. expressed that for what might come upon that upward path—oppression, social inequality, and generation of human cruelty—they had small regard, they looked to the end, and believed that it would be so good that the rest must be soically accepted.

Political changes in the 15th and 16th centuries contributing to a movement of revolt against authority and to an assertion of individuality. It is interesting to search out what it was believed this liberty would produce, and we may do it by exploring the works of those who have contributed to the democratic tradition.

1. The great theorists took certain claims for granted, not seeking to justify them, perhaps because they were considered sufficiently ultimate as values to be impossible of justification.
2. The values were stated by people who, as a rule, were not in authority but fighting against it, and were therefore obliged to discover or invent some rule to justify their revolt and their positive claims. Or, they were people who had acquired authority so recently, and usually by battle, they still had to continue to encourage themselves and their followers.
3. Almost all felt resentment against tyranny. Some, like La Boitie, were sensitive to the cowardice of people who lived under it, and compare their degradation to that of beast. Others, like Milton, inveighed against the result of a tyrant's power, terrible because it was 'boundless and exorbitant.' Paine said that the principle of kingship caused man to become the enemy of man since royal ambitious incensed them to hostilities.
4. The denial that anyone person or arbitrary grouping could be so certain of the righteousness of their values that control over their government was unnecessary. This tendency began with Lutheran doctrines and found its way, as a crude and non-rationalized enthusiasm, into the sermons and tenets of the new Non-conformist sects. They spoke of 'conscience', 'grace' and the light of nature, which informed

individuals and gave them a sovereign validity. But in the hands of men like Cromwell, Locke and Milton and afterwards of Paine, Humboldt and J.S. Mill, the red hot enthusiasms were moulded by circumspect reason into weapons less cumbrous, if at once more destructive of tyranny and constructive of liberty, in their fine logic. Cromwell urged "equality of conscience". Locke averred that every church is orthodox to itself: to others, erroneous or heretical. Whatsoever any church believes, it believes to be true; and the contrary thereunto, it pronounces to be error.

Stages of Democratic Development

There was a long way journey for reaching the end point of the ideological debate of the most fervent and better kind of government, i.e. democracy. Some important stages for development of present day used idea of democracy which are as follows :

1. *The Demand for Tolerance*—The first stage was the demand for tolerance of non-conformity in religion and the rise of self-governing sects like the Independence, the Separatists, and Presbyterians. They cannot be entirely identified with the middle classes and the small commercial men. In the American colonies, the small and middling people who had torn themselves out of the English agricultural background formed the center of the movement. The very rich and the fairly rich held with bishop and king; they were the nobles, the great landowners, and the governors of their counties. The peasants in all lands had sporadically revolted, and had been used by the Crown, the nobles, and the towns for their liberties; the day of the rank and file

was not yet, for while their leaders were organized, and disciplined, they themselves were not.

2. *The Demand for Representative Government*—In France and England the townsfolk led the movement for representative government. Their commercial and industrial interests urged them to make of the legislative, the executive instrument of numbers of people in close proximity and constant intercourse caused the growth of freer manners and a regard for the essential man. The French Revolution was its revolution although as in the English Revolution the poor of the towns and the countryside followed them, partly for the general benefits of free and settled rule. At a sad but perhaps unavoidable moment, the practical elaboration of the revolutionary principles was checked by the necessity of defence against the more feudal countries. Nepolionic genius was needed, but it converted France into a barracks, the opposite of a democracy, and later the forces of 'legitimacy' triumphed. The royal executive and the nominated council had fled, and government was conducted by elected assemblies' representative of agrarian interests. The separation of powers and check and balances suddenly became of vital importance to those who feared such movements, and Montesquieu was acknowledge to be to political science what Homer had been to Greek literature.

3. *The Demand for Universal Franchise*—By 1848 the interests below were already grappling with those above, but already a new element had entered destined to end the struggled by a victory for universal franchise, and to change the nature of democratic government. The peculiar economic claims of the working classes, arising out of the nature of factory, industry and the capitalist system, resulted in the conversion of the claims for a rather abstract

political freedom—the freedom of governmental negation or political dissociation—into the claims for economic equality. Further, the existence of the franchise for some citizens necessarily brought about an extension of it for all, for the enfranchised had different interests, and in order to win power by a majority of votes, they were bound to compete with each other for popular approval by campaigns of political excitement. They brought in outsiders to win their battles for them, just like the tyrants and parties in Athens, and the Catholics and Protestants during the wars of religion, and here as there, the strangers stayed, to become masters.

4. *Clarification through Conflict: Democracy*—The forgoing institutions of democracy we have listed and explained were proposed over the centuries by the pioneers of the democratic movement, some of them being more interested in one or more rather than all of them as being the most certain guarantee of what their authors wanted in the social and individual result of government. The years since 1917 have been full of a worldwide ideological debate of the most fervent and bitter kind, between the exponents and practitioners of Fascism, Nazism and Communism and the defenders of democracy in the countries of Western Europe and Western hemisphere. The result has been added clarification of the Lincolnian tenet that democracy is "government of the people, by the people, for the people".

Political participation in a democracy derives from the principle of equal rights and achieving the best in public welfare, and since there is no objective way of determining which particular individual might most acceptably discover and utter them, all are entitle to formulate their opinions with equal rights. This political equality gives the maximum encouragement to criticism of public official keeping them aware of popular needs, and desires, and obliging them to answer. Equality also encourages, because it flatters, popular leadership in political affairs. Under a dictatorship, equality of rights is excluded; participation means carrying out orders without questions. When it is said that democracy is right, it is asserted that all individual values deserve the rights to be heard and manifested them to attract attention and command themselves, it is right that the reconciliation shall be made by all voices equally heard. Values can be called 'interest' or the 'religions' of individuals or groups if it will make the matter clearer.

To some, democracy has meaning in the political field only, which regard as a form of government and stands for the rule of majority. Whereas to others democracy goes beyond the frontiers of politics, it goes to the extent of saying that it is also a way of life. What was originally a political principle has been enlarged to include social, economic and ethical ideas. Democracy, it is claimed, stands for an egalitarian society, in which the individual has equal status with others. There will be no difference between man and female, rich and poor. All will be treated in an equal way. As W. F. Willoughby says, "The word democracy is unfortunately used in popular discussion, and indeed in much political literature, in two quite different senses, as designating a society or community in which class distinctions are absent or relatively unimportant, and as designating a distinct form of government."[2] But in an egalitarian society the term equality is no substitute for uniformity. Afterall, equality is a matter of derivative value; it is derived from the supreme value of the development of personality— in each alike and equally but in each along its own different line and of its own separate notion. That is, the principle of equality needs to be adjusted to the values of man's functional capacity.[3] The idea of equality is more of a prescriptive than of a descriptive nature. Hence, the simple aphorism that "all men are equal" simply means that they should be treated alike in respect of certain fundamental traits common to all like their dignity and worth as human beings and not that they all possess attributes or capacities in an equal measure. With the increasing democratization of governments the fundamental problem has been to pull down the barrier of segregation and to offer equal opportunities to all. The aim of democracy has everywhere been to eliminate man made, socially fostered discrimination that has enlarged for some and restricted for others the avenues that lead to education, income and advancement. It does not, of course, mean a dead level of uniformity and a refusal to recognize the natural differences in character and intellect. Because of the "differences in the gifts which nature has bestowed on some and denied to others," natural inequality has been and must continue to be a fact in human society. Democracy is sometimes regarded as government by consent or by public criticism. In a democracy, one man or a group of men cannot rule as they please without the consent of the people, but governmental machinery has to move according to the wishes of the people and for meeting the requirements of the people. Government has to be responsive to public opinion, and in the light of genuine and responsive to public criticism, it may have to change its course for the benefit of the people. An unpopular and inefficient government, which has lost the confidence of the people, is likely to be overthrown by the pressure of public criticism and through the ballot box.

India, which accepted Western Democracy as models when it became an independent country, chose the democratic model as against the totalitarian path. The Constitution of India underlines the great importance of freedom and social welfare. Democracy shows hospitality to all kinds of ideas, and it is possible in a democratic state for several parties to function freely. In India, for instance, there is scope for plurality of ideas, and several parties exist.

Those who say that parties like the Communist Party should be banned in India, do not realize that one of the basic principles of democracy is freedom for all individuals and associations including political parties to function freely.[4] Democratic government implies the rights of free discussion and criticism to all the people, the right to form various parties and associations for propagating ideas freely, the freedom of the press, a liberal suffrage, periodical election, absence of privileges, full enjoyment of liberties and equality before the law. In a democratic state, people can criticize the government through various agencies of public opinion and even they can form different groups. Democratic politics can succeed only in a democratic society. In such a society there are democratic non-political associations. In a state where non-political associations do not allow liberty, equality, discussion, opposition and tolerance, the democratic political machinery cannot function. In a democracy the responsibility for making decisions regarding governmental personnel and policy rests ultimately with the citizens. It turns the social area into a vast reservoir of hitherto unknown political power. Conflicts in the social area create tensions which, in turn, raise political issues.

Present day society is pluralistic and dynamic. It consists of many vocational, religious, ethnic, linguistic, economic, cultural and other groups, each having particular interests, aims and aspirations. When any of these groups tries to bring any pressure on any branch of government, it becomes a pressure group. Thus there can be multifarious pressure groups, which organize themselves under efficient leadership. Whether the groups exerting pressure on government are good or bad depends upon the manner in which they function. If their activities are purposeful and wholesome, pressure groups form a good link between the people and the government and aid in the democratic processes.[5] The term 'pressure group' has come into use to signify and aggregate, organized or unorganized group which applies pressure tactics. It is defined as any combination of persons, bound together by shared goals and attitudes, who attempt to obtain decisions favourable to their preferred values by all means at their disposal but specially by gaining access to the governmental process. The first political scientist who paid much attention to the phenomena is A.F. Bently, who in his process of government speaks about the various pressures exercised by interest groups. Pressure groups also appear as normal usages in scholarly writings of the late 1920s like W.J.M. Mackenzie in his "Pressure Group—The Conceptual Framework." O.B. Truman in his "The Governmental Process" follows in the tradition of Bently and define it as "any group that on the basis of one or more shared attitudes make certain claims upon other groups in the society for the establishment, maintenance or enhancement of forms of behaviour that are implied by shared attitudes." A.de Grazia in his "The Elements of Political Science" defines pressure groups simply as any organized social groups that seeks to influence the behaviour of political affairs without seeking formal control of the Government. D.D. Mckean in "Party and Pressure Politics" speaks of pressure groups as an organization interested primarily in policy which do not ordinarily nominate candidates. The political character of the pressure group is particularly stressed by V.O. Key, Jr, "Such groups while they may call themselves non-political are engaged in politics, their's is a politics of policy in the main." R.M. MacIver in his definitional analysis of pressure group acknowledges as 'serviceable' the use of the term pressure group as denoting "any aggregate, organized or unorganized, which applies pressure tactics." Garcean and C. Silverman say, "All pressure groups must devise means for gaining access to and influencing those who are constitutionally empowered to make, administer or otherwise define the law." From the above statements of different thinkers, we can come to certain assumptions.

1. To begin with, pressure groups signify the existence of a group life. It is an attempt not of a particular individual but a group attempt, a concerted effort. This group may be an elite or teacher or student or proletariat or like other categories.
2. The most common denominator for all interest articulation is the sharing of attitude. Beyond their individual peculiarities men are conditioned by their group loyalties. Identification of man with a landed interest, a mercantile interests a moneyed interest with many lesser interest, grow up of necessity in civilized nations and divide them into classes motivated by different values. These common motives are in fact, the building blocks of the groups shaped by the interaction within the group, the experiences of its members etc.
3. Pressure groups cannot operate without formal organizations without which in average citizen are an innocent by standard and also a bewildered one. Organization represents concentrated power which can exercise a dominating influence in the political process. Institutional machinery like a secretariat or bureaucracy is necessary to see that the group attitudes are translated into resolutions and communicated to points of decision making.
4. The authors of the pressure group keep them away from law making functions. They are not law making agencies at the same time; they attempt to help the legislature to pass laws in their favour. It implies external inducement to control the behaviour of the legislators.
5. A pressure group comes into existence with a view to fulfil certain doctrines or goals. Further, the objectives which a particular group stands for should fit the prevailing patterns of values in the country at large.

6. An important feature of pressure group activity is the prevalence of democratic condition. The remarks of Madison, namely that the "Liberty is to function what air is to fire," means that pressure groups thrive in the lands of the free and cannot flourished under totalitarian conditions.
7. The question of leadership is another common feature. A group needs a leader to advance its claims effectively. He needs access to the administrators as well as legislators. Wide official contacts with the people who have intimate knowledge of the political process are the invaluable assets of the leaders.
8. The word "pressure" indicates the applications of techniques or methods of influencing decision makers. It is through the various tactics that the pressure groups get accepted their preferred values and gain access to the governmental process.
9. We can find out that a pressure group operates in order to get its grievances redressed by the government. This necessitates the action or response of the government. Pressure group tactics are futile if it fails to make a favourable impact on the government.

The existence of the pluralistic type of society in modern times means the presence as well as the relevance of the innumerable variables and their proper representation. The formal structures of the government as well as the party system have proved inadequate. On the other hand, a third approach of unofficial power has come into existence, namely the pressure group. Since, the government as well as the party system has not been in a position to focus problem areas, this third line of representation has necessarily come into existence. Democracy lives on responsibility and consequently, it requires sufficient openness about how political and administrative decisions are reached, so that the public may spot out undue influence and incase of any lapse it is corrected. Where they work in the open, pressure groups fulfil a necessary and potentially wholesome function.

With the study of pressure group, we can highlight those underlying forces and processes through which political power is marshalled and applied in organized societies, preferably on democracies. It, however, does not imply their total non-existence in a society having an authoritarian system for the simple reason that even in a totalitarian order such groups exist though they are highly circumscribed and thereby "serve merely as instruments of the state for securing ends which are state-determined, or they may become part of the façade of government for legitimizing decisions. A line of demarcation possibly subsists in the degree of involvement. A pluralistic society, with a democratic order, recognizes their existence and ensures widest possible participation to the extent of making them the principal avenues of activity out of the "official administration". A totalitarian order, on the other hand, encourages and permits them to work in a particular direction congenial to its own interests. However, the paramount fact remains that in every society, whether democratic or totalitarian, pressure groups seeks to influence public policy in a desired direction without being ready to accept the responsibility of public office as well as by declining to hold direct responsibility for ruling the country.[6] When men united into groups have their interests and use 'pressure' for the sake of their protection and promotion as Hagan points out, the life in society, in all its phases, can be stated in 'groups of active men'. The allocation of social values is done by means of decisions which are taken by diverse activities, each not being quite separate from each other, though the mass of activity, having common tendencies, in regard to such decisions, is manifest in the form of groups and interests. A study of group politics like, a newer wave in the direction of modernization of this subject, and though much more useful theories are yet to come, it is certain that the ice "has most decidedly broken".

Modern democratic governments of several countries have a close relationship between pressure groups and political parties. However, the intensity of relations varies from country to country. In France, for instance the relations between pressure groups and political parties are very close. Several pressure groups in France are subordinates to the political parties. But in many other countries the relations are not that close, and the degree of pressure group influence depends upon a number of variables. In a political party system, where party discipline is weak and powerful ideological differences are absent, the legislators are very much sensitive to pressure groups influences. Another determinant of pressure group activity is the complex of attitude orientations or what is called political culture obtaining in a country. American political attitudes show a greater political tolerance for pressure groups activity than is the case in European liberal democracies. Again, in some cultures as in France, direct action and recourse to violence by pressure groups may be common. In recent years in several countries the relations between pressure groups and governments have been institutionalized. In UK, for instance, there are advisory committees which contain the group representations.

Pressure groups are both 'natural and necessary'. It is natural for people with similar or identical interests to combine and put up a united front. Without organization, their common problems would not get adequate representation. The pressure groups retain a firm grip on their members and thus impose the much needed discipline. Pressure groups do not operate in a vacuum. Against every pressure group, there is a countervailing power. For instance, both the employers and the employees have pressure groups which keep the balance nearly even. Moreover, civil service, cabinet and the Prime Minister naturally put a brake to all unreasonable demands or pressure in Britain. Pressure groups help policy formulation; they are the barometer of various interests in the community. They represent the enlightened self-interest and also help the government in the implementation of certain important national policies. Even though pressure groups are not the parties which are not contesting in the election, but the target structure of pressure group involve the entire paraphernalia of a modern legislative organization beginning from electoral struggles to the point of policy formulation. Their role may be discovered in the writings of political manifestoes, distribution of election tickets and the formulation of legislative policy. Hence, the role of pressure groups, in this regard, may be discovered at three tiers— election; party; and parliament.

1. *Election*—These groups concentrate their efforts on the electoral system by helping agencies that may work to their advantage at the time of polls. It is accomplished by creating a strong and favourable public opinion for a certain political party and its nominees.
2. *Party*—They resort to the help of a party by contributing to its electoral funds and thereby winning tickets for their favourite parliamentary nominees. In such a situation they are successful in infiltrating their 'agents' into the legislative chamber for a more effective participation in the decision-making process of the highest representative body. But the outspoken role of these groups is manifest in the legislative organization where debates on important aspects of public interest take place and decisions are made in that respect.
3. *Parliament*—In a parliamentary form of government with a stable two-party system and in a land of

conservatism as the hallmark of national temperament like Britain these groups work in a more disciplined manner. Even in the event of grave dissatisfaction they don't shirk faith in the ethics and usefulness of peaceful and constitutional channels. When the groups maintain their association with one particular political party, they have a good chance of controlling legislative machinery in the event of that party's winning at the poles by a comfortable majority. However, in the event of strict party control through whips, they are not in a position to act haphazardly by pulling in contrary directions. But in America the case is different. In America, federation and separation of power have decentralized the whole political system to such an extent that, despite a stable bi-party system, pressure groups work freely for the sake of their instrumental objectives and, in the absence of strict control exercised by the party whips, resort to the practice of 'Pork-barrel' and 'log-rolling' for the realization of their objectives. More outspoken is the manifestation of pressure politics in the Senate where the device of filibustering is used to obstruct the proceedings for no other reason that the realization of some specific interest. Likewise, the device of gerrymandering is a shrewd way of redrawing electoral districts on the eve of elections for increasing the prospects of victory of the favoured nominees at the expense of the nominees of the opposition. However, in both Britain and the United States, pressure groups entertain moderate, secular and constitutional objectives in the legislative process. France, Italy and India present a different example. In these countries the groups are more expressive in extra-legislative sphere. In an attempt to influence legislative policy, here groups resort to many extra-constitutional, even undemocratic devices.

It is obvious that pressure groups desire to keep control over the legislative organ and for this the question of means, methods, and techniques engaged their attention. Again, the question of techniques is closely related to the system of political administration as well as the socio-economic conditions of the people. For instance, in very prosperous and advanced countries more stress is laid on propaganda and investment of money so that the legislative policy is controlled by them in consonance with their particular interests. But the same situation does not exist in a country having a system of proportionate representation inasmuch as the formation of hotch potch ministries puts a very heavy premium on the working of stable coalitions. The people of a culturally and also politically fragmented society choose their legislators in proportion that leads to the protection of local, instead of national, interest with the result that standing committees of the legislative assembly are colonized by powerful specific interests in many respects.

In a parliamentary system of government, pressure group seeks to influence the executive through legislature. Questions, adjournment and call-attention motions and votes of censure are the various devices through which the legislators induce, threaten or force the ministers to implement or stay a particular policy-decision in the light of the interests of their pressure groups. Ministers are, after all, elected by the people and electoral fight needs money as well as cadre support. Naturally a minister elected with the help of a group is hardly in a safe position to frustrate the hopes of his makers. Legislative support is required to pass a resolution, adopt a bill and carry through a budget inasmuch as defeat of an official motion amounts to a vote of censure. It is obvious that the ministers have to count upon the support of the dominant groups of the legislature in order to avert their defeat.

The establishment of several committees and sub-committees for advice and consultation by the departments' affords a very convenient channel for organized groups to promote their interests. Now every democratic state relies on the view that these agencies form a deposit of expertise upon the different aspects of policy which, effectively used, create an atmosphere of responsibility about governmental acts. If the minister acts upon their opinion, he is at least building upon a foundation of experience, if he rejects them, the creation of an opposition and, as a consequence, of the discussion that is the life-blood of democratic governance, is adequately assured.

A situation of inter-penetration of group and administrative activity can be seen in three ways:

1. *Advice*—In the name of technical and complicated matters faced by a department, various consultative and advisory bodies are formed either in pursuance of a legislative measure or of an executive decision whose basic purpose is nothing else than to facilitate acceptance of the agency's action by the groups represented on such bodies. However, the device of working through the committees is more a handicap than a positive advantage for the simple reason that the terms of reference are very limited and the recommendations given after any services deliberation are purely of an advisory character. The members of an advisory committee also feel short of total support from their group. Even if a group is well cohesive and its advices are given with a sense of unified conviction the department may not like to accept it in entirety or without hesitation for fear of opposition by other groups whose interest are adversely affected.
2. *Administration*— More useful for group interest is the device of administration. A situation characteristic of the occupational licensing boards and similar independent agencies comes to take place when one homogeneous pressure group is directly or indirectly

charged with the administration of a function. Then we have a more or less complete control of administrative action through the delegation of governmental power, especially rule-making power, to the organized interest group. Quite different is the situation where two or more conflicting groups share responsibility for decisions.

3. *Propaganda*—The device of administrative propaganda employed as a means of protecting the access of one set of interests and restricting that of others by altering their relative strength. An administrative agency charged with a highly ambiguous mandate by the 'labourers of demagogic leadership' is almost used to force propaganda in order to control access to its decisions. It is likely that the battle of propaganda may take the shape of a 'guerilla warfare' compelling the government to check its sinister development.

In a modern democratic society, the protection of specific interests through bureaucracy is a matter of dexterous mechanism of modern government. Legislative declarations are either very sketchy or controversial and it is the business of the administrators to convert them into a routine affair. For want of time as well as of necessary capabilities, the legislative bodies leave a work to be accomplished by the departments supposed to function under their control. The administrators then inherit a resolution of adjustment among conflicting interest with the mandate of implementing it within an area of operation. New grants of power are made by the legislative bodies to expand the stock of administrative activity. And again, when the legislature is confronted with an insurmountable difficulty of ample time and necessary expertise, the authority of the department automatically multiplies. The penetration of influence into the sphere of public services does not occur at the immediate level as we find in the cases of the legislature and the executive. That is, in terms of target, bureaucracy occupies a secondary place. The first target is the 'open' organs of government (legislature and executive) and the groups strive to exercise their influence on them as a matter of policy. However, their penetration affects bureaucracy when both the legislature and the executive fail to protect their interests to the extent they desire. In such a case, the activities of interest groups touch non-political branches of national administration and civil services happen to constitute a dominant area of their concern. Obviously, in such a situation, bureaucracy tends to be multi-functional by protecting and promoting diverse interests. As such neutral and independent character of bureaucracy is seriously affected.

The relationship between pressure groups and bureaucracy in a non-western country has its own silent aspect. Contradistinguished from the West, the penetration of influence in the civil services finds place at the primary or immediate level. Bureaucracy in countries of Asia and Africa lives like a congeries of diverse interests pertaining of same region, caste, language, economic status etc., and the groups do not look to it as a secondary target. Instead of using legislature and executive as their first or immediate target, the groups place more reliance on public services and, for this reason, bureaucracy becomes the dominant political party or a military junta where a single 'hero' having a charismatic personality is supported by a 'powerful elite'.

Pressure groups take part in electoral politics to induct men of their choice into the seats of political executive, their concern with bureaucracy is no less important. Administrative departments have an army of officers who are 'experts' and who control their 'lay-masters'. It is these experts who influence their respective heads at the time of policy making and decision taking. As such, it is they to which pressure groups count for an effective realization of their purpose. Political prudence informs that it is always judicious and profitable to look to the real masters placed in comfortable chairs than to those whose tenure is subject to shifty elections and whose wisdom, knowledge and experience are controlled by their subordinates. The field of appointed posts is always prone to expensiveness; the field of elected ones is narrowed by the war of nominations and the results of elections.

In a certain respect, even administrative agencies are like pressure group they not only administer what is given to them by legislative mandates but also act as originators of proposals for legislation and often exert an influence in the making of new policy. The civil servants have a tradition of their own and to budge from it is not an easy affair. It is wrong to say that they are just 'clay' in the hands of their masters (that is ministers responsible to the people in their elected deputies), since they often initiate movements leading to the formulation of a new policy which may sometimes run even the formulation of a new policy which may sometimes run even counter to the inclination of the party in power. It is found that at times they act as representatives of group interests and thereby exert their weight in matters of management of programmes of procurements and expenditure that significantly contribute to the fortunes of great economic concerns. Facts may be furnished to prove that vast aggregations of public servants animated by traditions, aims and interests have a major role in the political process of a democratic country. A degree of relationship between the pressure groups and administrative agencies can be established to prove that they are elements in the patterns of politics that may be jarred or re-aligned by the result of an election but are seldom completely thrown from power.

The penetration of pressure group politics into the domain of public services has its own ground of justification. Men conducting administrative services are not merely an inert mechanism to translate the will of a legislative body into action. They are living human beings like others engaged in various other fields of officials and non-official activities.

Thus, being a very powerful force in the political process, they play a very important role in the determination of what is to be done in the name of the state. Politics and administration are no longer separate things; they have become a unified discipline under the complex life of complete aloofness from administrative agencies. Conflicting interests, therefore, not only content for the penetration of their influence, they also prevent the possibilities of bureaucratic parochialism of the pettiest type.[7]

The penetration of the politics of pressure group in a judicial system of a democratic government is indirect. Judges are insulated from outside political pressures. The purpose must be served somehow and what the organized groups fail to get through the legislature and the executive, they desire it to be done through the judicial process keeping in view that judiciary is the ultimate guardian of the rights of the people and the protector of the constitution. Hence, the penetration of the politics of pressure groups into the judicial system is inescapable despite every possible arrangement of maintaining the independence of judges. The reason is that the judges are selected without regard to their political affiliations, that once selected they shall hold office for a long-term—for life, or during good behaviour, that shall not be subjected to dismissal by the executive may be removed only for misconduct as established by a formal process of impeachment or address on the part of both houses of the legislature, and that their compensation shall not be withheld or dismissed during their term of office. The selection of K. Subba Rao (Chief Justice of the Supreme Court who had earned repute in the opposition circles after his decision in *the Golak Nath Case* in 1967) as an opposition nominee for the Presidency against the official Congress nominee (Dr. Zakir Hussain) suggested the Government of India "to discriminate between candidates for judicial appointments on the basis of their social philosophy.[8] Another example in India may be furnished here to demonstrate the growing significance of bar associations in a move that was initiated to frustrate a contemplated step of some 'leftist' M.Ps for impeaching the two Supreme Court Judges who had given their verdict against the Government in *the Bank Nationalization Case* of 1969.[9]

An effective onslaught of public opinion is a very clever tactic in the hands of interest groups to influence the judicial process from a distance. The bombardment of personal or anonymous letters, dispatch of telegrams, picketing or gherao of judges etc., are neither desirable nor permissible to the public and all. But the creation of a strong public opinion becomes a democratic way of influencing the Judges. Collection of thousands of signatures in favour of acquitting an accused and wide publicity through the press can be cited.[10]

The role of pressure groups in the formation of public opinion is important affairs in the study of a modern political system. Three strategies of the pressure groups may be mentioned in this regard as suggested by Childs[11]—

1. Pressure groups use the strategy of argument to appeal to the minds as per the reasoning capabilities of their audience. They published annual and special reports, books, pamphlets, etc., and display pictures to argue their case. Religious, scientific and other empirical evidences are employed, speeches delivered, press conferences engineered, panel discussions held and a host of other similar arrangements made for this purpose.
2. They utilize the strategy of persuasion to arouse hate, fear, love or any other emotion that transforms intellectual conviction and acceptance into votes, attendance, purchases and loans. It is noticeable that everywhere groups are prompt and appropriate and applying whatever psychological, sociological or

other findings about human nature may serve their purpose.

3. They employ the tactic of publicity to call attention to their appeals. This device is concerned with the most effective use of communication media, not only of mass media, but of personal contact, small groups, local papers, bill boards, and radio and television stations.

Organized groups in a society compete with one another and find that the most successful method to build up influence and pressure in the realm of public policy, under a democratic government, is through propaganda or special pleading with these pressure groups, it is vital that the most important generalized power structure in society (government) explains its activities for the benefit of all the people. When partisan petition, have been heard, weighed and evaluated, and decisions made upon compromise among the whole spate of special pleading of all interest groups it is the responsibility of the government to publicize the decision and the reasons which support it.

Determinants of Pressure Group Politics

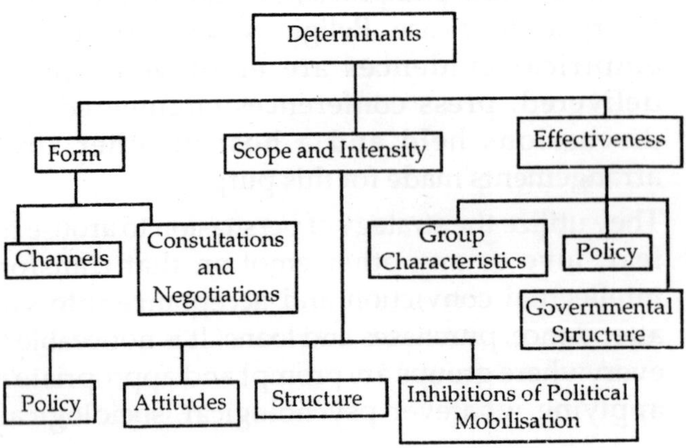

In a country with a parliamentary form of government pressure is mainly concentrated on the executive branch for the simple reason that parliament lives like a tool in the hands of ministers who, in turn, are a tool in the hands of their permanent officials. The characters of contemporary social and economic policies have become so technical that a lay parliament is no match to an 'expert' bureaucracy place behind the cloak of ministerial offices. Hence, the proper place where decisions are actually taken is not the 'open parliament' but the 'closed department' and, as such pressure groups concentrate their attention on the 'closed' branch of administration. It, however, does not preclude the possibility of exercising influence upon policy-making through members of legislatures who can use their political influence by means of asking questions, putting adjournment motions, making private representations and also utilizing the source of their prestigious contacts. Moreover, many groups maintain clandestine connection with a political party either by paying donations or rendering other kinds of assistance at the time of electoral contests. They just posed a condition of political neutrality in order to save themselves from the dangers of oscillation of power from one political party to another. In this way, pressure groups strive to have their prosecutors first in the party and through it in the parliament and, as the powers of a parliament have been usurped by the executive in every form of government, they seek to exercise their influence upon the ministers and civil servants for the sake of having a share in the effective power of policy-making.

Coercion or exercise of pressure by means of force is the ultimate weapon used by the individuals and their groups to secure compliance of their wishes and the acceptance of their demands. It is the nature of a reserve which is to be used when other techniques of politics of persuasion fails to serve the desired purpose. In order to see that specific interests are protected and promoted, as far as possible, pressure groups emerge "to protect, defend, threaten, inform, educate, and destroy and so on."[12] Hence, we may now study various techniques that are employed by the pressure groups in this regard. They are many, depending upon the temperament of the nation, limits of the constitutional provisions, availability of legal sanctions and socio-economic conditions of the people. There are four main techniques of pressure groups that have had their manifestation over the last few years— lobbying, bandh, strike, and gherao.

1. *Lobbying*

It is a favourite technique of the pressure groups operating in every political system, whether it pertains to liberal democracy or totalitarianism for the simple reason that politics is the struggle for power in which they play their part. That is, any group that makes claims upon other groups or upon the society as a whole finds it well-nigh impossible to stay out of politics. As in a strictly *laissez faire* system of the nineteenth century, the government had to provide the legal framework within which social action take place, so in a modern industrial society (where regulation extends in some degree to almost all human activities and relationship), the decisions of public officials are of crucial importance. They are and must be subject to the close and continuous attention of the groups they affect. Even the most authoritarians rule must take into account the army, the priesthood or some other politically influential eliments.[13] The existence of pressure groups and the use of the technique of lobbying is conspicuous in a free or open society where the obligation of the government to consult the governed is recognized and institutionalized through guarantees of freedom of speech, press and assembly along with the right of the people to petition the government for the redresses of their grievances. Thus lobbying occupies a preferred position in the constitutional system because it is necessary to the preservation of self-government.[14]

The operation of lobbying occurs mainly in the area of legislative activity in a free and democratic society. Hence, we first refer to the employment of this technique in relation to the organization and working of a legislative body. Here it signifies a very effective weapon in the hands of pressure groups to bear their influence upon the legislators. Its most sensational form is mass lobby. The object of this technique is to persuade the Member of Parliament of the degree of feelings in his constituency on an issue and incidentally to put some arguments to him.[15]

As lobbying is a technique of influencing the body of legislators, it may take any form such as personal meetings, delegations, and deputations to representatives of the legislative bodies, writings of letters and making telephone calls, sending cables and telegrams, making demonstrations, and so on. In addition, support rendered to the candidates at the time of electoral battles with men and money and threats of withdrawal of such support at the time of the ensuing election belong to this category. It is the constituency which provides the group with a sure way of catching the attention of the Members of Parliament, no matter an open display of such weapons amounts to the branch of parliamentary privileges is some respects. While withdrawal of support or its threat is no contempt of the House, the issuance of threat may amount to the same although the offer of monitory assistance in any form is certainly a breach of parliamentary privileges.

Lobbying in the form of electoral support to the contesting candidates is governed by the consideration of inducting 'agents' into the legislative chamber. Support rendered during electoral fights in the shape of 'open' manpower or disguised monitory assistance keeps the elected representatives virtually in the pocket of pressure groups.[16] However, the nature of the operation of this technique differs from one state to another owing to different constitutional systems and socio-economic conditions of the people. For instance, in a backward country having remnants of a feudal economy and torn by a multi-party system like India, lobbying takes the shape of violent manifestations as strikes, bandhs, gheraos etc. Moreover, as every legislative body works with the helps of committees where detailed considerations take place over bills and other measures of proposed legislation, lobbyists fix their mind on these legislative committees where they strive to have their colonized agents. While, in a rich country with a presidential system, working on a loose party organization, like the United States, lobbying plays a very outspoken and legally recognized part of the professional organizations.

A proper sanction to the practice of lobbying must be discovered within the framework of democratic government which recognizes every man's right to struggle freely for the protection and realization of his interest for the sake of national goods. As in every society some men are more assertive to make their rights meaningful than others, this has meant, in practical terms, that those interests with much to spend for protection have proclaimed "lobbying for all men" as an almost sacred article of faith.[17]

2. *Strike*

In very simple terms it was 'stoppage of work', which is the commonest pressure tactics in the hands of one party to coerce the other to concede its demand. However, as the stoppage of work cannot be done by a single person, it involves plurality of men with the same intent of compelling the other party to meet their demand(s) or grant a redressal of their grievances. Moreover, a refusal to carry on the work requires concerted action for the realization of their objectives. A statutory definition of the term 'strike' is thus given in Section 2(q) of the Indian Industrial Disputes Act, "Strike means cessation of work by a body of persons employed in an industry acting in combination, or a concerted refusal under common understanding or of any number of persons who are or have been so employed to continue to work or to accept employment."[18] As regards the nature of strike, it may be said to include three ingredients, namely, the number of men involved, effect resulting in the stoppage of work, and their combined endeavour to achieve their purpose. The tactics of strike cannot be employed by a single person inasmuch as it needs a concerted action of a group of men. The practical manifestation of a strike reveals stoppage of work in which the consideration of periodicity is immaterial. As such, a strike may continue for minutes, hours, days, weeks or months. But the purpose of the strikes cannot be achieved without concerted action appearing in the shape of mass 'leave' on some fake and flimsy ground, or the exercise of persuasion and force upon others to do likewise. However, a person on leave or absent on some other grounds may be said to have various types and forms as mentioned below:

I. There is a thing like 'sympathetic' strike. If the persons involved in it resort to the cessation of work in sympathy with their fellow workers with or without having any specific demand or grievance of their own pertaining to their economic relationship with their employers. Sometimes, the workers feeling reluctant to go on strike because of the 'fears' of hardships or consequences, resort to a 'token strike' which means stoppage of work for a very short duration though it may issue a warning signal about the shape of things to come. When the persons involved commit an act of strike with the object of forcing their government to adopt or scrap a particular form of legislative measure, appoint a commission of enquiry or dismiss a minister etc., it becomes a political strike.

II. When the area of striking activity covers the whole country or its major part and thereby affects 'key' administration as a whole, it is called 'general strike'. What we call 'bandh' is an instance of this type. Such a strike is generally undertaken by the workmen against all masters. It is not to be expected that an adequate number of workers will be animated by a sufficiently vigorous class conscious spirit to strike simply and solely for the purpose of terminating the capitalist system. What is wanted is a strike on the part of a sufficient proportion of the workers in key industries to secure the paralysis of capitalism. As there is no limit to human ingenuity the workers of a public utility or essential services may stage a new kind of strike variously called as 'regulation strike' or 'go slow strike' or 'work to rule strike'. It means workers being in place but adhering to rules and regulations in a very meticulous way really going against all canons of normal working behaviour.

III. There is a peculiar situation where we have a strike in the midst of no-strike. However, such a strike is different from its variety called 'pen-down strike', 'chalk down strike,' 'tool down strike', etc. In the latter case, the workers remain on duty without doing any work; they also refuse to vacate the premises of their work on the plea of 'being on duty' in a peaceful and non-violent manner. The salient feature of a sit down strike, in addition to refusal of work, is taking over the possession of the property of such business with a view to refuse access to others desiring to work. It is more a blockade of plant and machinery than of the owners. The strikers neither do work, nor leave their places, nor allow any of the persons to work.[19] Such type of strike is likely to take the shape of a violent activity as destruction of furniture, papers, machinery etc. amounting to criminal trespass and hence punishable under the criminal law of the land. The employer is justified in using even police force to get his premises vacated.

IV. The most reprehensible form of strike is fasting or hunger strike where a person stages *satyagraha* without taking any food or drink. Fasting is a religious ritual and, as such, it is considered a sacred way of self-purification. Under the law, fasting is a crime if undertaken to the point of starvation and death. But fasting in public in the name of *satyagraha* has got a political significant. Though the declared nature of fasting if often non-violent, it may tend to degenerate into an ugly situations of violence. The most pernicious aspect of hunger strike finds place in the declaration of a *satyagrahi* that after such period he would perform, self-immolation, publicly in case his demands were not met in a satisfactory way.

V. Take any form of strike, it is different from boycott and picketing, no matter both may often be seen in co-existence with it. Boycott consists of dissuading public from having any affinity for or connection with an offending employer in order to put him in a situation of serious loss. Picketing means posting of men involved in a strike near the place of work so that they may persuade, win over, or stop, even forcefully check, the non-strikers from resuming work or maintaining any connection with the offending employer. For this sake, dissemination of information by means of propaganda is needed to arouse favourable sentiments.

VI. It is strike that brings all groups of workers into a co-ordinate and co-operating class, intensifies their class consciousness, and cultivates a militant feeling among them. An economic strike becomes less the separate act of a special group of workers and more the act of a class fighting for the ultimate triumph of its formidable revolutionary aims. In this way, strike becomes a direct action for a general economic and social revolution, a weapon for forcing a general capitulation of employers and governors to workers.

VII. The technique of strike has certain dangers. Strike as Gandhian technique has its own justification in view of its being based on the forces of truth and non-violence; otherwise it is always a method of violence in the hands of the employees to coerce their employers. The work by means of affecting a concerted and organized stoppage of work in essential industries shows that it is the only sure means in their hands for compelling the dominant social groups to take action for the redressal of their political and economic grievances. Sometimes, the workers take the situation to the final extent of paralyzing the administration of the country that compass the government to take repressive measures. As a part of it different departments have different rules and regulations in connection with the working conditions of the employees of the respective departments and also take up different actions from time to time. For instance, in January 2009, ONGC has dismissed 64 officers across the country for taking part in the nationwide oil strike. In the dismissal order, the ONGC Director (Human Resources, New Delhi) said that the strike was illegal. "In spite of being made aware of the provisions of Rule 10 (b) of the CDA Rules, 1994 of the Company, under which no employee shall resort to or in any way abets any form of strike or coercion or physical duress with any matter pertaining to his service or the service of any other employee of the company...... Considering the circumstances of the case, it is not reasonably practiced to hold an enquiry.....Therefore, in exercise of powers delegated under Rule 41(B) and Rule 34 (VII) of CDA Rule, 1994, the undersigned (Director, Human Resources ONGC) imposes a penalty of removal of service," the order stated.[20]

3. *Bandh*

Bandh means 'closer' that, for the sake of convenience, may be likened with a general or total strike of all, whether offices, shops, markets, transport and the like. It is more sinister than a strike, whether partial or total, since it is a destructive technique of organized violence for any political purpose concerned with the toppling or formation of a government, weakening or strengthening of an alliance, humiliating and harassing the leaders in power or in opposition and the like. The instances of bandh illustrate that it is a mischievous device of enacting a managed riot involving mob-violence and mob-manipulation.

It is even identifiable with a civil war in some very extreme cases inasmuch as, despite all claims made by the users of is being a legitimate and peaceful and democratic affairs, it is the manifestation of a blind rebellion staged by political parties, pressure groups, students and others to obstruct, weaken, or overthrow the established order against which this pernicious technique is employed.

Bandh, as they have occurred in the form of violent disturbances in major towns of the country and as they have usually been staged by the Communist, Para Communist, fascists and their sympathizers, may conveniently be labelled as rehearsal of a bloody insurrection. That is, they have been wrongly construed as peoples resentment against the failures of the government on different fronts—whether language policy, food problems, rising prices, increasing unemployment and the like.

It should, thus, be borne in mind that bandh is certainly a very dangerous weapon devised in recent years. It is not at all a further extension of the Gandhian technique of strike based on the forces of *satyagraha* and non-violence. In its practical manifestation all the tricks may be conceived to have been employed and the frustration that most opposition parties must experience has added to its viciousness.

4. Gherao

It implies 'encirclement' or 'confinement' of the employers by the employees for coercing them to meet their demands as per their satisfaction. The main ingredient of this peculiar tactic lies in the confinement of the other party for any length of time. That is, it is a form of lock-in of management, employers or subordinates for houses and days until their demands are met.[21]

Undoubtedly, gherao is the most reprehensible technique of agitation politics and its occurrences cannot be justified even by the canon of expediency. Nothing but the storehouse of ruination—moral, mental, political, economic, social, cultural and psychological—is the net result. Gherao is not merely one crime, it is a bundle of crimes involving criminal trespass, wrongful restraints and confinement and a host of other wrong punishable under the penal law of a country. Its net result "is the proliferation of indiscipline all around." Persons involved in this pressure tactic are liable to be arrested without warrant and punishment with imprisonment and fine.

After having a proper study about the role of pressure group in a democratic country, it may be commented that pressure groups have opened a very wide channel of study and thereby broadened the scope of democratic values to include rather every association or group committed to the protection and realization of interest through governmental activity. But in the politics of pressure groups it is the shrewd and corrupt leadership which enjoys a position of special advantage. Then, the behaviours of these groups are hardly democratic either towards other groups operating in the society or even towards those which come to render their support on some occasions. The organization of leadership and other hierarchical units operate in the hands of unscrupulous persons indulging in quite selfish and irresponsible ways. Their game of hide and seek in politics brings about a situation of their difference with political parties with the result that they cannot be held to account for their policies, their leaders cannot be turned out of public office and punished at the polls. Though selfish and narrow interests effectively organize important and socially significant ones go unrepresented. Various pressure groups operating in a political society are viewed with moral indignation and alarm owing to their sinister penetration in the mechanism of modern representative system. It is further charged that the technique of lobbying as practiced by the groups constitutes a whole congeries of abuses, corruption and fraud manifestly weakening people's faith in the system of popular government. It is also contended that any degree of appreciation of the role of pressure groups in a modern political system becomes reminiscent of the Fascist Corporate state. Hence, it "may be said that the opinion representative significance of all organizations arising in connection with men's activities within the total context of modern industrial life has become sufficiently apparent to make it necessary to reckon them as pretenders to the throne of government. Where the interests are sharply divided, certain of these groups have proceeded to take over the government and to revolutionize it in such a way as to suit their particular needs and conceptions. Such efforts have been accompanied by dictatorial method—relapse into crude techniques of constitutional limitation.[22]

Even though the above objections are there, the utility of pressure groups in the working of a modern constitutional system cannot be neglected. Exponents of the group theory of politics and others subscribing to the school of modern pluralism emphasized the fact that there is an organic relationship between the individuals "are the heirs of the head, while the groups are limbs on which the body depends". If political parties are inevitable in the working of a modern democratic system, pressure groups have their own significance in the political process. Any fear of contradiction between individual and group political participation can be avoided by looking upon politics as a process rather than as a simple relationship between formal structures of a political system. It is unwise to purge or finish conflicting interests, rather the task "remains of distilling the general public interest out of the often—conflicting special interests which constitute part of the whole."[23]

It is quite clear that there is every need for keeping control over the interest groups in order to regulate their existence and working to the best possible extent. It is necessary to assure that; while making their contribution to the political process of a country, the groups are not allowed to lose their touch with their own member, or other groups of the society, or doing anything against public interest or general good. The case of public recognition of group participation caries with it the understanding that pressure groups conform to the same standard of political behaviour which is expected from the individual electors. It is quite true that the unorganized individuals at the ballot box have often become powerless to achieve anything in contrast to the highly organized lobbies with their direct access to the centre of power, but there remains nothing to prevent the state from reforming and regulating the pressure groups which exist and enjoy power without responsibility.

There are two main points of significance of the study of pressure groups in the political process of a democratic society.

1. They are numerous advantages to political parties and thereby contribute to the sustenance of the modern representative system. Power corrupts man and power alone checks power. The pressure groups thus act as a powerful check upon the arbitrary exercise of power and as they themselves are prone to abuse their share of power, it is essential that various pressure groups be allowed to act as a check

upon one another in order to establish and sustain the system of 'check and ballances'. It also implies that when the groups act as a check upon the government, the later must see to it that the activity of group politics is saved from deterioration to the extent of vitiating or destroying the political system itself.

2. The utility of pressure groups must be examined in the light of new approach to the meaning of politics. Politics is a struggle for power creating conflicts and offering their solutions and adjustments.

NOTES

1. Finer, Herman, *The Theory and Practice of Modern Government*, Surjeet Publication, Delhi, 1977, p. 68.
2. W.F. Willoughby, *The Government of Modern States*, 1936, p. 31.
3. Johari, J. C., *Contemporary Political Theory*, Sterling Publishers Pvt Ltd., 1987, p.294
4. Gokhale, B.K, *A Study of Political Theory*, Himalaya Publishing House, p. 269.
5. *Ibid.*, p. 393.
6. Grahaam, Wotton, *Interest Groups*, Englewood Cliffs, New Jersey, Prentice Hall, 1970, p.1
7. Merriam, 'Public Administration and Political Theory', in *Journal of Social Philosophy*, Vol. 5, 1940, pp. 305-6.
8. Quraishi, "The Presidential Election in India, In *Indian Political Science Review*, Delhi, Vol. II, Nos. 1 and 2, p. 37.
9. Johari, J.C. Lobbying in India, Independence of National Judiciary and Supreme Court Bar Association, in *Indian Journal of Politics*, Aligarh, Vol. VI, Jan. June 1972, pp. 39-55.
10. Johari, J.C. *Comparative Politics*, Sterling Publishers Pvt. Ltd., New Delhi, 1982, p. 366.
11. Childs, *Public Opinion*, Princeton, D. Von Nostrand, 1965, p. 237.
12. Turner, *How Pressure Groups Operate in the Annals of the American Academy of Political and Social Science*, Vol. 319, September 1968, p. 64.

13. *Encyclopedia Britannica,* Vol. I4, p. 175.
14. *Ibid.*
15. Stewart, J.D., *British Pressure Groups, Their Role in Relation to the House of Commons,* Oxford, Clarenden Press, 1958, p.207.
16. Berman, D.M., The Legislative Process in the U. S. Congress, in *Journal of Constitutional and Parliamentary Studies,* New Delhi, Vol. 2, No. 2, p. 41.
17. Roche and Levy, *Parties and Pressure Groups,* New York, Harcourt Brace and World, 1964, p. 192.
18. Johari, J. C., *Comparative Politics,* Sterling Publishers Pvt. Ltd., New Delhi, 1982, p. 399.
19. Aggarwal, A. P., *Gherao and Industrial Relations,* Bombay, N. M. Tripathi, 1968, pp. 14-15.
20. *The Times of India,* dated 12-1-2009, p. 1.
21. Johari, J.C., Gherao: A Pernicious Technique of Agitational Politics in India, in *Journal of Constitutional and Parliamentary Studies,* New Delhi, Vol. IV, No. 2, 1970, pp. 231-40.
22. Freidrich, Carl. J. *Constitutional Government and Democracy,* Oxford and IBH, Indian edition, 1966, p. 484.
23. *Ibid.*

3

Women's Organisation and Pressure Groups in Manipur

In this present day social scenario, women's issues no longer belong exclusively to the women's movement, if they ever did. This situation is especially visible in the world of development, and finds its clearest expression in proliferating references to 'gender' in local, national and international fora, among state functionaries, development experts, academics and activists—many of whom would not think of themselves as feminists—one hears repeatedly of gender bias, gender sensitization, gender planning and gender training to mention just some of the more common examples of its contemporary use. Women have the most immediate interest in, and are in the best structural position to begin to build, a progressive struggle that can affirm female associated reproductive concerns and values as the basis for a libratory integration of around our human needs and capabilities. In its articulation of these values, feminist struggle speaks to the growing potentials for an unprecedented libratory fusing of individual and collective self-development, of material and cultural production, of production and consumption (reproduction), of work and life, and of the personal and the political, in both its current practice, in both its current practice and in the new world to be created that is, as both means and end of a new politics. Changing and material conditions today, in which the motor of social development has extended beyond its industrial locus in the narrow production sphere to the whole of social life, have opened the political stage to significant participation by ever widening groups of people, transforming and broadening the definition of 'the people' in the process. Feminism is the cutting edge of that transformation, transcending and incorporating Marxism's earlier truths to reflect the values expressed in a broader popular struggle waged by a redefined and feminized humanity.

The practical realities of women's work and interests, then, as well as the fulfilment of the more abstract liberating potential of women's activism require that our politics be built from recognition is a far cry from its glorification. It acknowledges women's traditional association with reproduction and its values in the very moment of denying the necessity or inevitability of that special relationship, and refusing the oppression that it has institutionalized. It brings the specific perspective of women to the age old struggle of 'man' against domination, and in doing so posits a revolutionary affirmation and transformation of both radicalism and women's specificity, feminism articulates new and more universal truths—truths which end narrow single sex definitions of the world, and in the process, feminism and humanized politics.

Women, which have been relegated to secondary status is not only absolutely false but is the result of illicit generalization. The traditional Indian values expect women to be subordinate, altruistic and self-sacrificing. But the qualities needed in work place are competition, confidence and assurance. In Indian families, boys are encouraged and socialized in such a manner so as to develop masculine characteristics—aggression, dominance, independence, adventure and achievement orientation, whereas girls are encouraged to acquire feminine characteristics—such as submissive, nurturing, dependent and less achievement oriented. It is also true that girls are brought up for marriage as the supreme goal of life.

The customary laws of the various tribes of the region are always in favour of men. In the traditional society of Garo, women are ridiculed with a proverb "as a goat without teeth, a women lacks brain". The Nishis of Arunachal Pradesh possess wives as many as mithuns they have. The different Nagas believe that males possess six kinds of strength, females have only five and that is why, they christen boys on the sixth day after birth and girls on the fifth day. Moyon Nagas of Manipur consider that women have no permanent clan. After marriage husband's clan is imposed on them. Pre-marrital clan identity is not valid. The Zeliangrong Nagas have a taboo that man is not to sleep with wife or touch her inner garments before going to war or for hunting. It is an omen of bed luck. On the other hand, Zemie Nagas do not eat the meat of an animal killed by women.[1] Simply Manipuri Meities are saying that "How many sins have committed before birth that a woman can make?" It is sometimes argued that women are not allowed to participate in certain spheres of life. In no religious practices, whether Hinduism, Islam or Christianity, women are allowed to act as a priest. The religion has been the spiritual need of the individual and the society. The system of priesthood evolved as a functional aspect and then it established itself as a hereditary right of those born in priest family, and thus has continued to exist till today. It is a faith of dependency which has allowed this practice to exist. The Hindus depend upon Purohits in temples, the Christians depend upon Padaris in churches, the Mohammedans depend upon Mullahs in mosques, the Sikhs depend upon Granthis in gurdwaras, and so in each religion and sect we find the prominent existence of priest. The dictates of different religions has reduced the women to second class surrogate entity in the society. In Hindu, Muslim and Christian societies the women are treated as merely perpetuators of human race. In the Hindu system, the

Upanishad-Vedanta version has yielded place to Manu's code of life which relegated women to the lower hierarchy and considered as helpers on the path of *Moksha*. In the Muslim system, women are relegated to the status of procreators of the human race. The entire social and material relations are governed by this concept.[2] But there is certain exception in case of Manipuri society. The case of Meitei women performing religious rites and rituals in Manipur present a different picture no doubt. The traditional priestesses of Manipuri society are called the 'Amaibi'. They must be consulted for advice and *puja* on various matters. The Amaibis play a vital role in performance of rituals in temples and in the society. However, after the spread of Hinduism in Manipur the class of Purohits and pandits has also emerged. No doubt, the Amaibism is related to the traditional Manipuri faith which is still practicing and Purohitism to the modern Hinduism. The coexistence of both Amaibism and Purohitism is a peculiar nature of socio-religious aspect of Manipur.

Traditions and religions of the world accorded various statuses to women with different meanings. The Manu and the Islam have liberal attitudes towards women. But these also have clear dictates of subordination of women. Maybe such dictates were once formulated in certain social situations in which 'family' was regarded as a unit of society and its functions were given top most priority. Consequently, social stability was achieved but in the process women's status deteriorated. The common understanding was that if families do not provide security and protection in upbringing children and in particular the girl children, no other organization can save them. However time has proved this partly wrong when media often reported "families push minor girls into flesh trade". In some families birth of girl child is celebrated with the expectation that the girl will become an earning member after 10-12 years. On the other hand, birth of a girl is not a matter of joy in those communities and families where parents cannot provide security, protection, safety, food, cloth and education to the girl child.[3]

This is significant in the sense that while the traditional power structure does not give space to the women community to assert themselves, collective action and women agencies gave the space to them without facing any resistance from the traditional power structures. More interestingly, these agencies find a critical stake in the contemporary discourses on democracy in asserting their voices against the oppressive power state. This led to the emergence of a brand of feminism that, though critiquing the welfare state and its liberal social policy, holds that the gender imbalances can be overcome within the framework without reversing the structural prototype of the society.

Since the 1960s, the women's movement has grown from its origins in mainstream politics, the civil rights movement, and the New Left to become the most widespread, varied, and sustained social movement in North America. A large part of both its reform and its radical activity consists of pressure for women to have access to the rights, activities, and responsibilities commonly available 'to men', and to be 'let in' to full participate in all areas of society as it currently exists. For some, including some feminists, this adequately describes the totality of feminism programme.

However, most women's movement activism is based on a wider sense of feminism's project and significance. Many feminists' speak and act from a large sense of historical purpose in which their concerns, their forms of practices, and their vision represents a major break with the existing male defined world and politics. For these feminists solidarity among women—defining the world from women point of view, building women's autonomy as individual and as a collective power—is not merely the addition of one more 'constituency' to an existing radical politics nor only the articulation of the interest of yet one more special interest group. It is instead, a qualitatively new challenge to dominate by a group who relatively recent arrival on the political stage marks a major departure for progressive struggle in general. It is the articulation of these female and reproductive associated values that has provided the framework for her feminist project in general to move beyond simple pressure for women's inclusion in the world to become a full politics concerned with transforming the world.

The women's movement in India has followed the outline of similar movements in other lands but in some vital aspects, it has been different. The movement in England, for example, took a very strenuous course during which physical violence also played its part. English suffragettes their earnestness to obtain the right to vote, took recourse to unusual methods of securing the serious attention of parliament. They claimed themselves to railings in Westminster, they shouted slogans within precincts sacred to masculine deliberation—the House of Parliament—they took out processions, held mass meetings and resisted policemen, who came to restore 'law and order' which, to these women, was synonymous with the *status quo ante* of women without citizenship rights. When they were arrested and put into prisons, they went on hunger strikes and were subjected to the indignity of being forcibly fed. It may be interesting to maintain here that Lord Pethick Lowrence was one of the few Englishmen of vision, who actively supported the suffragette movement and his wife Emmelion Pethick was one of those prisoners.

Nothing like the English struggle fell to the lot of Indian women partly because Indian women were encouraged by men social reformers and leaders like Gandhi and Nehru. Other social reformers like Raja Rammohun Roy, Swami Dayananda and Swami Vivekananda and others took up cause of women and several laws enacted to improve the position of women. Religious reformism also started at this time. Raja Rammohun Roy (1772-1883) who can also be described as the father of Indian Reformism and Nationalism established the 'Brahmo Samaj' in 1828. Madam Blatavasky and Dr. Annie Besant started the Theosophical Society in Madras in 1879. The nineteenth century can justifiably be termed as the period of reform movement for emancipation of women, while the eighteenth century was the darkest period of women's suppression and oppression in India. The two movements that went side by side in the nineteenth century, were—(a) social upliftment through the abolition of existing customs like, the suttee, child marriage; and (b) female education.[4] After independence Pt. Nehru, the then Prime Minister of India, followed the steps. In the first Lok Sabha (1952-57) of free India, only 43 women contested and 14 were elected (out of a total number of 489). In a letter to the Chief Ministers (8th May, 1952) Nehru said, I have noticed with great regret how few women have been elected. I think we are very much to be blamed..... Our laws are man made, our societies are dominated by men and so much of us take a very lopsided view of this matter. We cannot be objective because we have grown up in certain grooves of thought and action. But the future of India will probably depend ultimately more upon women then the men."[5]

The other social reformers like R.N. Tagor, Iswar Chandra Vidyasagar, Swami Dayananda Saraswati and so on, supported him and launched movements for the betterment of women. They made persistent efforts for the introduction of female education, remarriage of Hindu widows, prevention of child marriage, and removal of polygamy. Consequent upon these efforts the widow remarriage act was passed by the government in 1856 even in the face of bitter opposition and raging controversy from the orthodox people.[6]

The participation of women in the Independent Movement resulted in the legal struggle for women's right in the championship of Mahatma Gandhi. After the independence, the Constitution of India granted the women equality before law and equal protection under the laws. Women were allowed legal equality in all respects except family laws. The marriage and family were not included in the Constitution as done in Japan and other countries. Because of this, the women in India still suffer. She is put under brackets of being a Hindu, Muslim, Christian or Parsi women.[7] Further, the battle in India initially was not so much against male domination as against the forces of superstition, apathy and ignorance, they crushed the spirit of men and women alike. Several decades after feminism breached many barriers around the world, Indian women are still denied the unchallenged right to choose. So, the domestic responsibilities, which remain the same for housewives and women who worked outside the home. Looking after the children and the house are considered the women's responsibility even though she may work the same hours as her husband in the offices. Amerdeep Sing, Associate Professor of English at Lehigh University, Pennsylvania, USA, defines feminism as a basic truth—women as human being too and entitled to equal rights. "I don't have to stand in demonstrations carrying placards denouncing male chauvinism," he says, adding that he tries to express his respect for women in quieter ways. This statement clearly expressed the meaning of feminism. It is not a movement for female advantages. It is a movement for justice and equality. The same thing that feminist do—a world in which relations between men and women are egalitarian. Men's pro-feminism is like any other set of values, beliefs or political activities. It comes from personal experience and other ethical or political involvement. Pro-feminist men are not anti-male. He is anti-sexist, anti-patriarchal but not anti-male. A pro-feminist man is hopeful about both men's and women's future.[8]

Internationally the 'question of women' and the growth of feminism are woven together with the history of nationalist movements which are demanding equality and free government. First wave feminism emerged in many countries in similar ways. In the early decades of the 20th century there were visits of European feminist campaigners to the Third World, for example, Ellen Key, Annie Besant and Margaret Sanger while Third World women made reciprocal journeys. The domain of second wave feminism had an even wider sway than first wave feminism. Feminist campaigns are inevitably shaped by national priorities and national politics.[9] In case of India, the contribution of women in the nationalist movement was not small. Women organized themselves into groups and were willing to join processions, face police firing and go to prison. They broke the salt law, picketed shops selling liquor and foreign manufactured cloths. There were women who joined terrorist groups and helped in editing and distributing banned newspapers and in manufacturing bombs. While evaluating the Gujrati women's response to Gandhiji during 1920 to 1942, Aparna Basu commented that it was an impressive record.[10]

The women's movement in India, therefore, has had a contribution to make, through women to the regeneration of a country which was suffering under the multiple ills of foreign domination, poverty, ignorance and an entirely out modelled social order. This had been a tremendous task especially since women themselves have been the worst victims of ills.

For the overwhelming preponderance of evidence from the social and behavioural science is clear: women and men are more alike then they are different.[11] Gender difference is the result of gender inequality, not its cause. Gender inequalities produce difference, and the differences produced are then used to justify inequality. The simple concentric acceptance that man's activities are more human and important than women's, however, soon began to be breached in all areas of feminist thoughts and activity. Opposing gynocentric construction of reality began sporadically but persistently to affirm women's specific culture and values, in a challenge to dominant notions of what is valuable in life. For instance in 1970 Barbara Burries wrote, "All the female culture traits are defined as negatives by the dominant world culture. We do not believe them to be so (except, those that keep up subservient, such as passivity, self-sacrifice, etc.). We are proud of the female culture of emotion, intuition, love, personal relationship etc. as the most essential human characteristics. It is our male colonizers—it is the male culture—who have defined essential humanity out of their identity and who are culturally deprived."

Traditional progressive values such as equality, dignity and freedom are central to women's struggle, but to limit the conceptualization of our politics to these existing parameters is to deny its deeper revolutionary implication. Feminist's politics must extend earlier progressive values in ways that reflect the transforming presence of women on the political stage. We are not simply entering politics as it has existed. When fully half of the human race has been excluded from the practice and definition of politics, our entry necessarily transformed its very shape and definition. Women's entry into politics as women is, in fact, the emergence of the long subordinate, devalued and marginalized sphere of private life and reproduction into the public and is an event of world historical significance. Any significant increase in women's participation and power in politics and production will require a concommitant change in the organization of the domestic sphere. Work there will not simply disappear. Even if it is shared equally by men, women's presence in the paid labour force without major social restriction will mean a significant additional workload for both men and women. As it, if the burden is not shared, the additional load has fallen almost entirely on the shoulders of women. We have, to be sure, marginally reduced our economic dependence because we now have access to half wage for the two jobs we do. But this is not liberation and will never seem so to women. The power and powerlessness of the women made up a changing cycle, depending on the status of her husband, her possession of son, her fertility, looks, health and capacity for domestic labour. The middle-aged mother of grown up sons could be a powerful matriarchy and elderly mother-in-laws could command and oppress young wives. The women would get more securely stitched into the fabric of lineage, caste and class at a later stage in her life cycle. We tend to absolute male and female domains—this is so in much feminist writings—and see them as seamless blocks, forming opposites of total power and total powerlessness. Patriarchy, however, operates through for more complicated trajectories, with crisscrossing power lines that fracture both domains and that, at times, unite segments across the blocs. The same women, depending on the presence of sons, her husband's status and fortune, and her age, gets to know both subjection and rule. This is why, and how, perhaps, women are, much of the time, complicit subjects of patriarchy.[12] Women sacrificed everything including their lives. The higher the sacrifice, the higher the salvation became a motto for women. In reality, women rarely had an identity apart from that given to them as wives, mothers and daughters. Although, they were worshipped as deities at home, they were treated as second class members of the family. Some historians felt that it was happened because of the fire which tied the women to kitchen, while others—think that it was due to needed protection of foreign invasions. Another reason supported is the patriarchal system where girl is to leave her parent's place and go to her husband's place. The girl being alone in the new family, it becomes easy to subject her with various atrocities.[13]

Since its inception, UNESCO has endeavoured to promote equality between men and women through action in its field of competence. While its primary focus has been on providing literacy and education programmes for women and girls, much attention has also been given to developing policy guidelines and advisory services to Member States on how to overcome discrimination of women and girls in areas of the Organization's competence. UNESCO was thus among the first to cope already in the 1980s with the complex issues of prostitution and trafficking of women and girls, the portrayal of women in the mass media, seminal works on eradication of sexist stereotypes in school textbooks, violence in the mass media, and other.[14]

Work on these topics was often on ground-breaking pioneering importance, but was later, unfortunately, placed on the sidelines or even abandoned. Moreover, although rarely mentioned explicitly, UNESCO's work has been fundamentally geared to implementing The Nairobi Forward Looking Strategies for the Advancement of Women, the objectives of which are still valid. In 1994, an evaluation was carried out of UNESCO's action concerning women and gender equality covering the period 1988 to 1993.[15]

The corrective or substantive approach recognized that in order to distribute benefits equally between women and men, approaches to promoting women's rights must transform the unequal power relations between women and men in the process. For this to happen, policies, laws and programmes must aim to provide the following :

1. Enabling conditions, in the form of the basic social, economic and cultural context within which women may be able to lead their lives with dignity;
2. Affirmative action in the form of temporary special measures where women's needs are specially recognized and catered for in the context of employment, education, financial services, politics and all other spheres of life in order to enable women to overcome barriers that are historical or those that arise from male domination in the system.

While social change may come at a price, it is often for more sustainable and long transformatory in the long-term if it represents a move from dependency to autonomy. The challenge is to know when to take note of difference, and to decide an appropriate measure for different treatment that will facilitate equal access, control and equal results. Such measures will have to be assessed to ensure that they promote autonomy rather than protection or dependency. This has to be done without compromising the claim for equal rights and equality as legal standard. For example, there can be no compromise on the claim for legal equality in matters pertaining to personal status such as : (a) citizenship and nationality; (b) rights within marriage and family relationships; (c) rights over children (guardianship); and (d) equal treatment before the law.

If women are to recognize their interests in feminists positions we must attack the privatization of domestic labour, its invisible and unremunerative nature and the fact that it is largely women's work challenge to the oppressive divisions between public and private life, between leisure and work, and between reproduction and production, is an integral part of feminism's resistance to the subordination and marginalization of reproductive activities and in male-dominated industrial society. More and more feminists are affirming these values and concerns as the central organizing principles of a new, more integrated, less fragmented and less hierarchical society. As a political perspective rooted in women's specificity begins to emerge within feminism, we can see how its emphasis on the simultaneous integrative transformation of the fragmented public and private realms of life opens the ways and culture. It is this that provides the basis for the clear expression of feminists' sisterhood as the affirmation of women together, rather than the threat to women that its enemies (liberal, radical, and right wing) point it to be.

In the post-1975 period women's organizations conscientised the wider society, worked with all classes of women, combining developmental activities with mobilization for socio-economic rights, put a limited but successful pressure on the state for legislative action to curb exploitation of women in matters relating to marriage, rape and workers' right. They raised many questions specific to women and challenged patriarchal values in all spheres and structures through agitation tactics, propaganda and lobbying. Many problems of women are class related. Therefore, while separateness as a gender-based movement was regarded as essential to unify women vertically and horizontally, collaboration with other socio-economic and political movements was also seen as necessary. The women's movement joined civil rights movements, struggle in rural areas, people's and workers movements. It challenged state policies on population, women's employment, environment, training and organization of women workers, planning for rural development, agriculture, education and so on, and protested against atrocities against women distorted portrayal of women in the media, and so forth. As a consequence of all these activities, the movement grew increasingly political. Their concerns have shifted to such basic issues as the state of the polity, the state of the economy, the criminalization *per se,* violence and the rise of fundamentalism.[16] Conscious of their political rights and Western democratic values, these women worked actively to generate political consciousness among women during the early decades of the 20th century. They took up the issues of voting rights for women with the Secretary of the State for India, Lord Edwin Montagu, who was in India to discuss the demands for political reforms. The South Borough Franchise Committee was initially reluctant to give women the right to vote but because of the sustained campaign launched by women organizations and the support given to them by the Indian National Congress and other political parties, it was finally left to the provincial legislatures to decide the matter. Madras was the first province to grant the Franchise in 1920 followed by Bombay in 1921. It was, of course, extremely restricted and when the first provincial elections were held, less than one per cent of the female population could exercise its right to vote.

The refusal to extend the purpose of the movement to a general attack on the existing social structure, and the identification of social reform with continuation of British rule had, in fact, brought the movement to an impasse.

The process of women emancipation gathered further momentum during the later years of freedom struggle under the leadership of Mahatma Gandhi and others. The 'modernist' context of the freedom movement as a struggle for national independence and the creation of a democratic and secular state, carried on an appeal for the liberationist aspirations of Women bound down to family and social bondage. Gandhian ideology provided the moral legitimacy for the women's cause. This was true not only for the rural uneducated women who belong to Gandhi's 'constituency' but also for the small section of educated women who were organizing themselves under the auspices of independent women organizations, such as All India Women's Conference (AIWC) founded in 1927, the Indian Women's Association, 1917-37, and the National Council of Women in India (NCWI) founded in 1925. These groups advocated women's rights to franchise, educational opportunities, and social reforms, including such radical options as abortion. Among the powerful myths generated in the course of the freedom struggle, the most effective was women's participation. The self-defined and self-directed participation is true only for the small number of Indian women who joined the independence movement under the banner of women organizations. However, a large number of women particularly rural women were also mobilized; that is, drawn into the struggle through a predetermined programme under the charismatic and paternalistic leadership of Gandhi.[17] Even though women typically slipped back into housework and anonymity each time the tide ebbed, the possibility of asserting themselves on a larger scale was engraved in their memories. For a limited number of educated young women, programmes of economic and social development undertaken during the Five Year Plan periods provided possibilities for employment and, to some extent, self-determination. Although the number of females counted to shrink, opportunities multiplied for them in government agencies, business offices, bank branches, telephone exchanges, schools at all levels, hospitals, airlines, newspaper offices etc. Rapid expansion of higher education brought into being a corps of thoughtful and articulate young women serving as Instructors and Readers in Colleges all over the country. Emigration of men for jobs in the Middle East gave thousands of villages as well as cities wives responsibilities previously assumed by their husbands for management of family, finances, planting and harvesting of crops, dealing with merchants, many leaders, and public authorities. Everyone's right to vote opened up another space, in which a hand full of women became prominent in political parties and achieved ministerial status at national and state level. Both foreign funded and local development oriented associations, popularly known as NGOs some of them specially committed to 'empowerment' or 'conseeintisation' of women proliferated.[18]

Patriarchy may remain the dominant mode of social organization but over the years, the plurality that is hidden under it has led to the notion of patriarchies. New material from different regions of India gives evidence of this plurality. One must add that the modernization process in the early twentieth century has also made an impact on the making of femininity. Western feminist theory initially tended to portray all relations between the sexes as sites for exercise of patriarchal power. Despite this recognition of plurality, the notion of women caste, as including all women exists in popular understanding as for instance in the Marathi Phrase *bai chi jat,* literally meaning the caste of women. There is perhaps, a submerged feminist consciousness that caste keeps women away from a truer understanding of patriarchy.

Overcoming material obstacles is indeed of prime importance but neglect of transformation of values and attitudes can subvert the libratory potential in these endeavours. Education for women instead of promoting greater autonomy may become an additional attribute of marriageability; independent earning merely end up as additional responsibility undertaken for the family, often to support an unemployed husband or to support their children and others, with male members abdicating their responsibility, participation in public affairs can result in being tools for some one else's agenda.[19]

Even after 60 years of Independence, India is still not liberated enough. Though India has today captured the attention of the world, and is among the fastest growing economies, deep rooted ancient beliefs continue to dominate our lives. An overwhelming majority of Indians, rich or poor, long for a son because they believe that they can attain *nirvana* or go to heaven only when a son performs funeral rights. So a daughter is never so welcomed as a son. Then there are issues of dowry. Investing in the education of a girl child is perceived as something that has no return. These socio-cultural factors constrain women, more so in the rural and semi-urban areas, besides reinforcing a negative self-image. Collectively, this outdated way of thinking puts a severe brake on the progress of the girl child. The falling sex-ratio is indeed a cause for concern. It is, however, heartening that government is trying to bring down barriers against girls in education through various schemes such as the Kasturba Gandhi Balika Vidyalaya. The scheme addresses the issue of gender disparities in rural areas and among disadvantaged communities. These residential schools for girls from underprivileged sections are indeed a breakthrough in the education of the girl child. The protection and care of the girl child is a challenge that calls for a four pronged strategy—

1. There must be strict enforcement of the Preconception and Pre-natal Diagnostic Technologies (PCPNDT), Regulation and Prevention of Misuse Act. We must make sure that offenders do not get away. Government and NGOs could work in close collaboration to help implementation of the law. There is also a dire need for legal literacy.
2. Through advocacy we can build public opinion and work towards a mass movement for stopping the practice of sex selection. We must express our absolute contempt and shame against such genocide. Punit Bedi, an Obstetrician and specialist on foetal medicine, has said in a recent article "More than 6 million female foetuses have been killed in 20 years". That is the number of Jews killed in the holocaust.
3. Enlist more women in all developmental programmes apart from education. Make them economically independent. Once they have disposable income, they will be seen in a different light. Today a number of women are employed, but it is only the tip of the iceberg. This despite government, through the national policy for the empowerment of women, endeavouring to create an environment for the development of women.
4. Promote youth icons and role models such as Sania Mirja, Sunita Williams, Barkha Dutta, Kiran Mazumdar, Kiran Bedi, Mallika Sarabhai, Indra Nooyi, Meena Borwanker etc., are to name just a few. They are all achievers, and they are all women. While they came from urban India, there are hundreds of women who have done remarkable works for tribal and village women.

The point is that nothing is impossible for women. More and more women wisest realize this. This can happen by changing societal attitudes and community practices through active participation and involvement of both men and women. The women are represented as having emerged from the home only to be assailed by doubts of a new kind, all of which serve to exteriorize her. If earlier, her role as homemaker caused her to locate her identity in the smiles of the people, she worked so hard to please, today we see her identity residing in how pleasing her external appearance and activities of any kind is to the people who matter. The idea of a woman outside home was imbued with a sense of opportunity and a desire to make something of her life through the dint of her efforts. With time, we see a gradual reversal of meaning attached to the idea of being outside.

Asians have always had the reputation for holding their women in low regard. Empowerment of women makes for good seminar topics here, but in real life, it's the men who decide their role in politics and public life. Indeed, some urban women have managed to create space for themselves, but in most parts of rural Asia, Western feminist theories do not apply—for they have different concepts of power and prestige systems here. But ironically, it's the South and Southern Asian Regions which have thrown up numerous women leaders who have led their countries in the last 50 years or so. In fact, the first women prime minister in the world was from South Asia—Sirimavo Bandaranaike of Sri Lanka who came to power way back in 1960. That was the beginning. It laid down the emotional track, which carried all the subsequent women leaders of the region to the most prominent political position in their respective countries. From Indira Gandhi to Benazir Bhutto—the first woman to head on Islamic country—to Mayawati Sukernoputri, the first woman President of Indonesia, the list is long and we are still counting.

Studies have revealed that only 14 per cent of parliamentarians in Asia and just fewer than 14 per cent in the Pacific are women. But even though their members may not be big, the expectation is that women's involvement in socio-politics improves the standard of governance for they focus more on development, are less corrupt and more sensitive.

A study done in Australia a few years back found that 54 per cent of that surveyed believed women who enter politics were motivated by altruistic and community welfare concerns compared to only 13 per cent among men. A good number (64%) felt men were motivated by personal interest and power, composed to only 11 per cent of women. The general feeling is women are outsiders in politics so they are better equipped to transform things. The failure of a politician is not based on gender; it's to do with the polity and the political culture. For example, in Sri Lanka and Pakistan neither men nor women leaders have been able to deliver. Similarly, both Nawaz Sharif and Bhutto were accused of corruption.[20] Different experts and intellectuals are giving different opinions regarding the power and activities of women. In Sri Lanka the society is paralyzed, leaders have to take hearse measures, which will make one part of the society unhappy anyway. And this has nothing to do with the gender of the leader, explains a Sri Lankan strategic expert. Experts say there is a novelty factor about women in politics, so expectations are high. They are seen as mother figures that are not very competitive and less cynical. But when in power, the system begs them down so don't expect them to do better than others.

Moreover, a women's tenure is revived more harshly than a man's. That's because there are more men in politics. A few analysts feel the bias against women come through when you put them on a pedestal and expect them to behave in a predetermined fashion. By assuming they are motherly, one makes them unidimensional. It is a predetermined simplified and narrow definition. In the final analysis, success as a leader has to do with an individual's drive and the ability to stand up against odds. Successful leaders have shown us this. Girls, and women from West Bengal and Assam are being trafficked to states like Punjab and Haryana where they are sexually exploited until they bear a male child, a United Nations report said on Wednesday.[21]

The source of demand driving the trafficking in young women arises from the gender inequalities in densely populated countries like India, namely the perception that a girl child is an economic liability, it said. India is simultaneously a source, transit and destination country for women and children trafficked for the purposes of sexual and labour exploitation. The existing patriarchal system and the resulting unequal status of women render the women vulnerable to exploitation, trafficking and HIV. Unequal gender relations leave girls and women with little choice or decision-making power regarding education, occupation and marriage. It also means that they have no power to negotiate safer sex practices, which increases their risk of HIV infection.

Over the last 30 years the sex trade has become worldwide. This process of industrialization in both its legal and illegal forms generates profits amounting to billions of dollars. It has created a market in which billions of women and children have been converted into sexual commodities. The sex industry previously considered marginal has now come to occupy a strategic and important position in the development of industrial capitalism. This particular aspect of globalization involves an entire range of issues that are crucial to understand the world we live in. These include economic exploitation, sexual oppression, capital accumulation, international migration and unequal development, racism and poverty. Traffickers carry out recruitment drives in the select camps through false promises of jobs in big cities. Interviews by the NGO's field teams with 60 teenage workers in Dimapur revealed that most of these girls were forced to join prostitution after similar false promises made by the traffickers.[22]

Prostitution often combined with trafficking, increases in the context of international interventions. Further measures are needed to prevent trafficking and the sexual exploitation of women in the context of peacekeeping operations. All missions have clear instructions to thoroughly investigate any allegations of sexual exploitation or assault by any peacekeeping personnel and to ensure that offenders are duly disciplined. The most serious problem of the present day Manipuri society is the issues of women becoming the worst victims of insurgency and counter-insurgency problems. Women are abused, battered, molested, raped, murdered, forced to commit suicide etc. Protection for the women victims and punishment to the guilty are ignored. The women become the victims of the armed forces wrath. Two sisters, Laishram Bimola (32 years) and Laishram Manishang Devi (29 years) of Pukhao Ahallup Awang Leikai, Imphal East were picked up by the CRPF on 14th January, 1999 at around 11 a.m. on charges of giving shelter to the underground activists. They were stripped off and were inhumanely beaten up by iron rods and stick on their hips, buttocks, thighs, calves and feet in the army camp of Pangei.[23]

On August 1990, the armed personnel patrolled party raped Smt. Ahanjaobi Devi of Takyelpat in front of her family members. The army personnel entered the house at about 3 a.m. and started body search on the family members. Ahanjaobi tried to run out of the house but those army men called her insdide and threatened that had she not entered the house they would shot down her husband and son. When she entered the house her husband was carried out and she was left senseless.[24] Many rape cases by the army go unreported due to fear of social stigma and state inaction towards the culprits of the armed forces. Ch. Jamini Devi an 11 year old girl was taken to custody by 32nd Assam Rifles station at Yairipok on the charge that she was the girl friend of an underground activist. She was interrogated at the army camp. The recorded version of the girl's statement was broadcast at a public meeting convened by the Commander of the Assam Rifles post. Two days later, on 2nd April, 1999, the girl committed suicide, being unable to bear the public humiliation.[25] The women's issue can be adequately addressed only through social movements both at the regional and national levels. The National and State commissions for women cannot be expected to do much because they function under the authority of the state which in turn operates under the dictates of international organizations that are least bothered with the women's issues. At present women do not even enjoy the basic rights enshrined in the Constitution. In India women activism is registered in the historical struggle for nationalism, worker's right and present struggles. In the North East the women have a rich history of movements in the insurgency affected areas. The collective empowerment and organized movements for common cause is the need of the day. The collective movement of such nature requires not only organization at the local level but also need network organizations at the national and international levels. Women's movement could countervail the state power. There is a real need to show organizational strength for making the state to take proactive role in favour of women. Insensitive way in which the state addresses movements was also seen when a case of attempted suicide was lodged against Medha Patkar when she sat on fast to protect against the raising of the level of the Narmada Dam.[26] The women's movement challenges the police and judiciary primarily as patriarchal structure of power and reshapes the potential of a powerful community of women who would in turn be tied against an unjust social order. This applies the North East too and the women's movement in the region needs to become also a part of similar movement at the national level. We should remind ourselves that compartmentalization of issues of concern should not be carried too far. Very often the issues of women also implicate the children and the young people. The displaced men and women are very closely related. Hence women's movement ought to be coordinated with all the similar movements that aim at securing equal rights of men and women.

With reference to the need of classification of movements by changes they intend to bring about Mukherjee suggests three divisions—Social movements, revolutionary movements and quasi-movements.[27]

(a) *Social movements*: Any collective mobilization for action directed explicitly towards an alteration or transformation of the structure of a system can be properly understood as a social movement.
(b) *Revolutionary movements*: When the collective mobilization aims at affecting wide ranging and far reaching changes in the major institutional systems comprising the whole society, we can rightly term it a revolutionary movement.
(c) *Quasi-movements*: Collective mobilizations aimed at changes within a system are quasi-movements.

The impacts of the above mentioned movements on the development of the women's movement needs to be assessed in North East India generally and especially in Manipur.

Mass movement is a characteristic of modern mass societies and it refers to the large scale participation of masses in organized political activity. The impersonality which isolated individual from the social order may bring other sections of the populations also in mass movements. Mass movements appeal to the emotion of dissatisfaction with existing political and social systems by their revolutionary ideologies they attract people from all classes who have their own scores to settle with the existing social and political system.

In the process of modernization and development the industrialists or capitalists are trying to influence political and economic policies. The government is pressurized from industrialists, landlords, peasants, workers etc. Any government is unable to meet equally the demands of all groups in the face of the existing and persistent clashes between various organized pressure groups which find their reflection in the political network also added with political corruption are retarding normal life and healthy production. Bottlenecks of efficient production, man-made difficulties, loss of working days, faulty allocation of priorities, faulty implementation of land ceiling laws, faulty location of industries which are all the results of this clash act as impediment to economic development of India, discontent and dissent are the regular features of Indian polity today. Lack of economic development and lack of consensus among the various pressure groups question India's ability to sustain democracy.[28]

In Assam and the entire North East India, there has been an unprecedented surge of popular anti-state movements. There have also been the democratically organized popular movements for state autonomy in Meghalaya, Karbi Anglong and Boro areas in Assam. The participation of women in popular mass movements goes without saying, particularly in the North East where women are more actively involved in economic and social activities. One of the prime contributions of the women's movement is solidarity which transcends barriers of race, locality, caste and to some extent class also. These differences are huge but a major premise of the women rooted as it is in the patriarchal structure of society which is also ultimately responsible for the caste and class system. The whole issue is very complex and facile generalizations are out of place, but it seems that contrary to feminist assumptions that gender discrimination is the key issue, it is felt that gender identity takes second place to current socio-economic issues. The larger women organizations and parties are naturally subservient to the interests of the parent party or women's organization, and though there is a lot of talk of independent women organizations this does not in practice work out. It seems that women as a group have yet to develop the organizational and managerial skills to sustain any large organization or movement on their own and totally independent of men. In the North East women are forced to be subordinate both from external pressure of the men-folk to conform to the community norms as well as due to lack of self-confidence. This may sound paradoxical in the North East, in states like Meghalaya and Manipur whose women are economically and educationally advanced. But in fact there is a strong tradition barring women's participation in politics in both these states which consequently have a poor showing of women even in conventional electoral politics. There have been strong women's movements for instance in the Nupilan Movements and later the anti-liquor and anti-drug movement (Nasha Bandi) in Manipur but these have been primarily social rather than political in nature, without a modern sense of political identity. The tradition of Meitei women's powerful civil society organizations rising against oppressive measures of the state and also against social evils is quite evident even today. In recent times they have been agitating against the Armed Forces Special Power Act operating in Manipur.

Women's movement in Manipur was mainly of the norm oriented type that is in connection with reformation. They, however, also involved 'value orientation', since social movement is multi-dimensional by nature. In the history of women's movement in Manipur, mention may be made that quite a few Maharanis took active part in the administration during monarchical period. The king as well as the people sometimes sought the opinion or support of the women to solve difficult problems or situation which affected the interests of the community. In the history of Manipur there were many evidences where the king took the opinion and suggestions of their Maharanis in matters which were of public interests. Sometimes women in a group gathered and complained to the king for correction, if he acted unruly and had done any injustice.[29] In most of these cases the Monarch very often changed the policies as requested by the womenfolk in order to promote the welfare of the society.[30] Raja Paikhomba (1666-1697), could not appoint Ingallei as Rani because people of Manipur refused to accept her as their Rani. The voices of the masses came so to think that Maharani was not merely the wife of the King but also the queen of the people and therefore acceptable to them. Above all she must be an example to them. The Maharani should be a model woman so that women in the kingdom might copy her.[31]

First Nupilan (Women's Movement 1904)

After 1891, Manipur was defeated by the Britishers at Khongjom War. The womenfolk of Manipur were very much agitated at the oppressive measures of the British authorities. A bad impression for the British authorities was in the minds of the Manipuri women after hanging Yubraj Tikendrajit and Thangal General. When the Yubraj Tikendrajit and Thangal General were hanged in 1891, some 8,000 or 10,000 women crowded round the scene of the execution. Whenever injustice was done either by the king or by the officials a group of women used to go to the palace and reported about the injustice and the authorities were also always compelled to correct their mistakes. Though they were not given political and administrative responsibilities, but whenever the authorities committed illegal acts towards the innocent people, they came out and fought for justice.[32] But women's movement emerged in a more organized manner with a creative ideology from the early part of the 20th century. In 1904 an agitation of the womenfolk of Manipur was compelled to prepare, for a fight against the injustice of the British. For the Britishers, the issue was quite political but for the women of Manipur it was a matter of socio-economic issue. But one of the most outstanding features of the issue was without the appearance of women in the scene; the issue was in a never ending condition.

The Colonials disarmed the whole population of Manipur, employed the Manipur army men as unpaid coolies to fetch rations from Khajuma in Naga Hills, 72 miles south of Kohima, for the British troops stationed in Manipur. The nearby villagers were made to work without any payment. Manipur had also to bear 50 per cent of the costs of construction of the road.[33]

The main causes for the outbreak of the Nupilan of 1904 was twofold— (a) The resuscitation of the Lallup which had already abolished by the same officer and (b) Wrong charges and imposition of unreasonable orders for punishment of the male members of the society.

After midnight, on the 15th March, 1904, the state bungalow, which was occupied by Captain Nuttall and Mr. Dunlop, assistant to the Political Agent, was burnt to the ground. The fire commenced from the verandah roof of the building and there was at the time a great suspicion of incendiaries. Again after three and half months, on 6th July the Khwairamband Bazar which contained 28 sheds with a seat capacity for 3000 market women was completely destroyed by fire. The destruction was so quick and although the air was quite still it was certain that the fire started in several places at the same time. Then in the night of 4th August, 1904 the bungalow lately purchased by the state from Mr. Mitchall, executive Engineer, and in the occupation again of Captain Nuttal and Mr. Dunlop was totally destroyed by fire.[34]

Upon receiving information from Mr. Dunlop, Maxwell, Political Agent immediately issued an order on 12th September, 1904, and submitted it to the Cherap Court for promulgation of the inhabitants of Imphal.

ORDER NO. 17

Manipur, the 12th September 1904

On the night of 15th March 1904, the Assistant Superintendent of State's *bungalow* was burnt down and incendiarism was suspected. On the night of 4th August 1904, the *bungalow* lately belonging to Mr. Mitchell, Executive Engineer, which had been purchased by the State and was occupied by the Assistant Superintendent of the State, was again burnt down, and this time there can be no doubt that an incendiary set it on fire. A reward of Rs. 500 was offered for information leading to the conviction of the guilty person or persons, but without any clue being obtained. As a preventive measure and proper punishment I consider it necessary to temporarily resuscitate *Lalup* in the town of Imphal for the purpose of rebuilding the house last burnt down. With this order are enclosed:

1. List showing the chowkidars' beats in Imphal; and
2. List giving the materials required for rebuilding the house, and the Chirap Court is requested to apportion the work among the several *Lekhais,* exempting no one but the *Rajbari,* foreigners, members of the Panchayat, and Chirap Courts and State servants. The State Engineer will arrange to take over the material collected and supervise the rebuilding operations. (*Sic.*)

H.St.P. Maxwell, Lieut.-Colonel, I.A.,C.S.I. Political Agent in Manipur and Superintendent of the State.

In the afternoon of the 27th September some 400 Manipuris came to the residency and they presented Maxwell a petition asking him to cancel his order of 12th September. Maxwell returned the petition to the Chirap Court next day for intimation to the petitioners, and said he was unable to alter his decision, and if the people declined to obey the order, the only alternative was to post a punitive police force on the town as a punishment for incendiarism.

After Khongjom War of 1891, the Government of India ordered the removal of the ruling famiy of Manipur from the Chieftainship of the state, and selected Churachand for that position. The Chief Commissioner of Assam got the information of the resuscitation of the lallup system by the Political Agent of Manipur, which might not have been judicious, but he ordered to arrest of any ringleader including the much agitated Rajkumars of the Imphal Valley. The trouble was evidently political and the outcome of opposition of Raja Churachand, according to the opinion of the British authorities. At this stage the people were not ready to accept the orders of the Political Agent, held meetings and protested. The British authorities also took up any sort of measures for controlling the movement, using more forces, issued orders like more persons, than five assembling in one place for the purpose will be considered an unlawful assembly etc. They also arrested six persons as ringleaders of the movement on 5th October 1904. But since the ringleaders were arrested and other prompt measures taken, their followers were totally disheartened and all opposition had ceased and people started asking for pardon. Rush was made to carry in material for the Bungalow and half the available supply was already collected in the first week of October 1904.[35] Pandit Bindu Madhob, son of Kosheswar Sastri, Manipuri Brahmin of Imphal asked the people to obay the order of the British authorities. He also appealed to the people to collect subscriptions to carry out the work.[36] The British authorities constituted a court from 4-11-1904. All the persons who were supposed to be the ringleaders of this agitation were also summoned and asked them to give their explanation to the Court. Thus after having all the necessary informations and evidences, Maxwell finally accepted the allegations against these six accused Rajkumars for organizing the assembly against the prohibitory order of the authority. On 10th November 1904 Maxwell issued an order to expel these six Rajkumars from Manipur. The repressive measures of the

British authorities had severely demoralized the people. And having no alternatives, the able male people of Imphal began to subscribe the building materials and prepared to rebuild the houses which were destroyed by fire.[37]

Whether or no, political or otherwise, the women were led by the simple thought that their husbands had refused to undergo the lallup labour which now became an illegal one, and thereby causing the hardships of punishment on the women's lot. Both the men and women of the country thought the British *Persona non grata,* and, moreover, the Political Agent had exercised powers regardless for the prevalent customs and traditions of the Manipuris and he certainly endeavored an interference with the existing institutions. The inconvenience caused to the innocent people of the Imphal valley was much regretted and despised by the working women and it were they who made strong protest against the orders of the British government.[38]

During this time, the real feelings of Manipuri women towards the Imperialist forces erupted with a true colour. They were compelled to prepare for a fight against the injustice of the British Imperialism. Thousands of women of the bazar came out spontaneously under the leadership of Smt. Irengbam Ongbi Sanajaobi Devi of Nagamapal Lamabam Liekai, Smt. Leisangthem Kwathabi Devi of Thangmeiband, Smt. Laishram Ningol Juboti Devi of Nagamapal etc. They began to launch a big demonstration and entered the residency to see the Political Agent and Superintendent of the state. As result, Khwairamband bazaar was also closed. The demonstration of the women continued for several days. The agitation became so serious that it began to affect the day to day life of the state and so even the government decided to import army from outside. The women's movement has had a contribution to make, through women to the regeneration of a country which was suffering under the multiple ills of foreign domination, poverty, ignorance and an entirely outmoded social order. This had been a tremendous task especially since women themselves have been the worst victims of these ills. In his diary of 5th October 1904, Maxwell wrote down a VERY SORRY REMARK as regards Manipuri women like: *"It is very difficult to know how to treat a mob of wild cat like this, but I shall take care to disperse them next time before they became numerous."*[39]

With that feeling of Political Agent, it was quite clear that the activities of Manipuri women during 1904 were a quite remarkable one. Although the duration of the agitation was very short, yet it produced a very good impact on the political and economic life of the country and also paved a way for the future anti-Imperialist movement which instilled the feeling of nationalism in the minds of the Manipuri people against the British Imperialist forces.

Second Nupilan (Women's Movement 1939)

People of Manipur solemnly observe 12th December every year as the 'Nupilan Day' to commemorate the heroic protest movement led by the Meitei women in Manipur against the decision taken by the Durbar with the influence of the Political Agent and Superintendent of the State, Major Maxwell of exporting rice from the state. In the pre-colonial period, the major part of the internal trading activity was managed by the Meitei women who had their exclusive markets located at Imphal. Under the Rajas, volume of external trade was very small. But under the British-Manipuri Trade and Defence Agreement of 1833 restriction of trade between Manipur and British India was relaxed. After 1891, when the British suzerainty was established over Manipur, the former pressured the Manipur Durbar to permit export of rice which was earlier prohibited.[40]

Class exploitation of the valley Manipuri's by the Marwary traders had already begun from the early decades of the century; but none of the Manipuri's took great concern over the matters. As the years rolled by and the number of population ever increasing the valley people of Manipur steadily realized their feelings of discontent against the Marwari traders who had now come out in the open to hoard every available foodgrains at very low cost from the ignorant villagers. Rice was the staple foodgrain of every Manipuri, but the production and scarcity of rice depended entirely on the timely rainfall or shortage of it. Flood, insects, amount of the hoarding by the Marwari merchants and the exports of rice by the state officials, for use by the British subjects at Kohima, Sadiya and other places in Assam were more or less responsible for the rise of price and the scarcity of rice in Manipur. People could not make any complaint to His Highness the Maharaja who himself took an extreme interest in the export business of the Marwari traders, when the ominous signs of scarcity became imminent.[41] The rate of rice export was increased year after year.

Year	*Export of rice (mounds)*
1897-98	11,106
1898-99	36,436
1922-23	80,000
1925-26	1,55,014

As a result of the export of rice, the price of rice was increased a lot, e.g. Rs. 3.14 annas in 1921-22; Rs. 3.11 annas in 1926 etc. Under the name of the Government contractors a number of Marwari merchants exported huge amount of rice to outstation like Kohima, Sadiya and Dacca Battalions of the Assam Rifles. All the Government Contractors were Marwaries. Their names and stations supplied are given below.[42]

The high price of rice had resulted with intolerable hardships of the poorer sections of the community. The first indication of the scarcity was the great increase in the number

Name of Contractors	Station Supplied	Quantity per month Maunds
Sudasukh	Kohima Battalion	1,000
Sooresh Chinder	Sadiya Battalion	1,000
Sanairam	Dacca Battalion	500
Badri Narayan	Dacca Battalion	300
Kaluram	Piphima PWD Coolies	80
Kaluram	Kohima Hospital	50
Murlidhar	His own shop	30
Ganesh Lal	Sadiya PWD Coolies	980 (One time only)
Ganesh Lal	Sadiya PWD Coolies	360 (For two months)
Jibanram Premsukh	Piphima Shop	200 (July only)
Sudasukh	Kohima Civil	800
Kaluram	Piphima PWD Coolies	900
Kaluram (For small Contract)	D.C. Kohima	3,000 (One time)
Deven Narayan Tiwari	Piphima PWD Coolies	450

of persons who came to seek reief in the poor house attached to the Civil Hospitals.

The outburst of the women's uprising of 1939-Nupilan second was so sudden, but it had a long socio-economic and political background. Different movements from different sections of people were there from time to time. The core problem of that time was the British Indian policy of impoverishment through the Raja of Manipur. Rice was the staple food grain of every Manipuri, but the production and scarcity of rice depended entirely on the timely rainfall or shortage of it. Flood, insect, amount of hoarding by the Marwari merchants and the export of rice by the state officials for use by the British subjects at Kohima, Sadiya and other places in Assam were more or less responsible for the rise of price and the scarcity of rice in Manipur. A brief survey of the annual fluctuating price and the amount of rice exported annually outside the state would indicate an outline of the economic conditions experienced by both the villagers and the townspeople during the financial depres-sion period of the 1930s.

Total amount of export

Total export of rice ———————— 372,174 mds, 37 seers.
Total export of chira ————————198,558 mds, 32 seers.

Out of which the following quantities were supplied for the government purposes

Kohima Battalion——Rice 8308 mds. 26 seers
Kohima Civil Jail——Rice 405 mds
Kohima hospital——Rice 389 mds, 18 seers,

The Marwary and other traders began to set up rice mills. They purchased the paddy as much as they could get, milled it and exported it outside. It is recorded that the milling agency of the Marwary traders and the bad harvest further added the suffering of the people. Administrative Reports of Manipur on December 1939 said that one Aribam Chaobiton Devi from Tera Keithel organized a small group of about four or five women of her own business circle and tried to stop the bullock carts which carried paddy for Marwary traders. They requested the cart drivers not to sell paddy to the Marwary traders. And they also requested the authority to close all rice mills on 12 December 1939 at forenoon, about one thousand women of Khwairamband Keithel (market) gathered at the market. From there they went to the office of the Political Agent, Gimson.[43] The movement was in a well organized and systematic one so the mighty Britishers were difficult to control the movement in an easy way. Maximum agitators were market women, doing small trade and commerce. This was because the scarcity of rice in the market directly affected them. Leadership was in the hands of these women who could present their views in a systematic and lucid manner.[44]

Although the immediate cause of the women's uprising was economic in nature, there was also a strong feeling of dissatisfaction with the State Administration over the Mangba-Sengba (Pollution-Purity) scandal of the year before 1938, and the long suppressed feelings of various taxes on the poor public by His Highness Maharaja. The fact that the Maharaja was the head of the Brahma Sabha caused a loss of confidence in the Administration.[45]

The State Administration of Manipur was conducted by His Highness the Maharaja and the Political Agent through a Darbar Members (30 ordinary and 3 Additional) were nominated by His Highness the Maharaja and most of them had 'near relation' with His Highness. The Durbar reserved three important state functions, in their hands, viz., Administration, Legislature, and Judicial. They decided cases of both Civil and Criminal natures. The Durbar was the highest court in the state and appeals from the Durbar lay to His Highness only, who got the power to decide the appeals in consultation with the Political Agent. *No appeal could go to any higher authority against the order of His Highness's Revisional Court*. There were two other subordinate courts known as the Chirap and the Sadar Panchayat Court, the members of which were all nominated by His Highness and who had 'near relation' with the Maharaja. Most of the Members were illiterate (they even could not write their own names) and extremely loyal to His Highness. The public was totally ignorant of the income and expenditure of the state; and the Resolutions, which were approved in the sitting of the Administrative Durbar, were not made known to the public, who, however, were made responsible for those resolutions. The public had to carry burdens of many taxes from various sources like—land revenue, road, fisheries, forest toll station, grass mahals, water cycle, vehicles (lorry), foreigners income, wakheisel, mangba-sengba, pandit loishang (for marriage purpose), sentek, pach-naped, chandan senkhai, kumjensen, tax for singers etc. All the taxes were not added to the income of the state; and some were meant for the private expense of His Highness and other state officers.[46]

As a result of the petition submitted by a number of villagers asking for an immediate stoppage of the rice export, an Administrative Durbar was hurriedly arranged in the early hours of the 12th December. At that time the Maharaja of Manipur was out to Nabadweep in Bengal for pilgrimage. The women agitators compelled the President to go with them to the telegraph office and get a telegraphic order from the Maharaja. The women also prevented the Commandant of 4th Assam Rifles who had arrived there for controlling the mob.[47] The number of the crowds were also increased gradually and reached about four thousand. The women repeatedly insisted that the approval of the Maharaja was not entirely essential and then the people became excited. Sharp tried to convince for some hours. The women then confined T.A. Sharp, Major Cummins, the Civil Surgeon, Major Bullfeild, Commandant of the 4th Assam Rifles with some other officials in the telegraph office and refused to allow them to go for food also.[48]

On 12th December 1939, Mr. Gimson was in camp in a Kuki village about 6 miles from Sugnu, which was about 40 miles south of Imphal, when his ASI of Police arrived and told him that there was a strong agitation in Imphal against the export of rice, and that things were looking ugly. Mr. Gimson got back to Imphal about 3 a.m. in the morning of 13th December. When he was talking to the crowd of women at about 1.30 p.m. (13th) a telegram arrived from His Highness the Maharaja asking him to help in the stoppage of rice export. Orders were issued at once stopping it, and Mr. Gimson thought that would satisfy the women crowd. But there were still the gathering about and he suspected further trouble. He arranged with Major Bullfeild to have the troops ready. Mr. Gimson was given information that the troops had to turn the women out of the telegraph office compound on the 12th and women were injured and some were even hospitalized. Mr. Gimson wrote in his confidential latter to the Secretary to the Governor of Assam: "21 women and one Indian Officer and 7 other ranks of the Assam Rifles were injured. All were treated on the spot by the Civil Surgeon and three other medical officers were present. The injuries to the troops were caused by stones. Some of the women were injured by stones thrown from the back of the crowd and others by rifle butts in resisting the troops. There was not any bayonet, although the troops had fixed bayonets." (Confidential No. 3872-G.A, Dt Imphal, The 26th December 1939 from C. Gimson Esq., ICS, Pol. Agent in Manipur to the Secretary to the Governor of Assam, Shillong).[49] The women now claimed that all the rice mills should be closed down.[50] On 14th December crowd of women started to march towards Mantri Pukhri where one Marwary run rice mill. But Mr. Gimson got there before them by car and after a lot of talk, in which threats of smashing up houses and the boilers were freely used; the women crowd had finally dispersed about 3.30 p.m. when the main fuses were removed from the buildings. The women were all quite friendly to Mr. Gimson personally; but the temper of the crowd seemed worse than 13th December. Mr. Gimson was of opinion that the agitation was wholly a 'women's affairs' and men and boys were round the outside. The agitation was mainly anti-Marwari which were instilled in the minds of the women from different sections of people a long time. Rice was much dearer than usual and owing to the mills the women had lost their small earnings from husking paddy. The main bass was genuinely economic; but some of the agitators had certainly taken advantage of the situation. In the meeting held on the 13th December about the embargo on the export of rice, severe and open criticism of His Highness the Maharaja were freely uttered. No incident occurred on the 15th December 1939 but in the afternoon a crowd of women came and presented a petition to Mr. Gimson asking that they should wholly received all the rice contracts and such other things. It was not certain whether the women would returned to the bazaar sooner or later, but upto that date (15th) Mr. Gimson could not procure any evidence from the Manipuri side as regards the unfortunate incident of the Telregraph Office of 12th December, and he had to talk to Major Cummins, the Civil Surgeon about the incident but the latter was away treating on Lindsay Smith at Kohima. It was quite clear that the activities of the women agitators were true and systematic, even though the administrators and the businessmen tackled the situation in a very tricky way. As a response of the tricky attitude of the businessmen and the administrators, the women did not stop their movement before getting the final solution. They were asking for closing the rice mills.

On 28th December 1939 some carters came to sell rice to the Marwary merchants in the bazaar in the British Reserve. The women crowd seized them and took the carters to the State Thana and had thrown some of their rice in the gutter. The carters made complaints to the Political Agent who ordered the carts to be brought to his Thana and handed over to the carters. He also ordered his Police to take a case. The Assistant Sub-Inspector of the Agency Thana asked the State Police to produce the women accused (5 of whom were named) so that he could record their statements. Thus on the next day (29th December), the State Police called the women in a crowd (very foolishly); but the crowd refused to produce the five women in public and said they (accused) would all give their thumb impressions. This happened at dusk of the 29th December. The crowd made strong protest saying that the Inspector of the State Police (Khomdram Dhanachandra Sing) had caught hold of one of the women crowd, slapped and kicked her and that a Brahmin woman was knocked down without mercy. Actually the Inspector of Police was secretly confined in the State Thana and the Police Member was also there. The women crowds were all round the Thana Office and they immediately demanded a Bichar and the Blood of the Inspector. While the women were thus in an ugly mood again His. Highness the Maharaja away for three days on a Shikar Expedition! Mr. Gimson promised to the crowd that he would send a messenger to the Maharaja at once and ask him to come back to hold a Bichar.[51] as a consequence of the irresponsible and neglected attitude of the Maharaja of Manipur, the women demanded a Bichar by the Political Agent and said openly that they did not want any decision made by the Maharaja.

The Political Agent, however, refused to hold any Bichar that night (29th December), because he felt sure that if the Inspector came out of the Thana Office the women crowd would have tried to kill him. Technically the State Thana was in the British Researve, which made things rather awkward. Maharaj Kumar Priyo Barta Sing, the second son of His Highness was the Police Member as well as Ordinary Member of the Manipur State Durbar, and he asked the Political Agent not to bring in the Assam Rifles to which the later agreed. During the night, both Mr. Gimson and the Police Member did not get any help from the President of the Durbar who had gone out to Yairipok, 14 miles away, after he received news in the morning that the women there had burnt all the goods of Manipuri shopkeepers. Later at 10 p.m., the women crowd had dispersed and the Inspector next day on 30th December. The Political Agent advised the Police Member to send the Inspector away for few days under cover.[52] The government believed that the cause of the movement was related to the administrative lapses in the State. Robert Reid, the Governor of Assam asked the Maharaja to make some considerable reforms in the administration of the State so that the intensity of the movement could be stopped. He further instructed the Maharaja to make a determined effort to grapple with the situation before it worsened.[53] His Highness the Maharaja had stopped the rice export and the rice milling system for some time, but the other demands of the public were not given due attention. On the other hand, the Political Agent left all the urgent matters of the State to His Highness, and the later, on his part, did not take up any prompt action to satisfy the demands. The helpless publics were in utter confusion because even after repeated requests made to His

Excellencies the Viceroy and the Governor of Assam they did not show any favour by preparing to interfere in the administration of the Manipur State. The public wanted them to constitute a Special Tribunal to enquire into the matters and to decide the pending cases. The Manipur State Durbar on the other hand, tried to decide the cases against the objection of the women mass who did not desire to see the partial and anti-prudent decision of the Durbar Members who were already declared unworthy and unfit of administration by the masses. It was openly stated that the Maharaja and the Political Agent were not interested in forming a Tribunal to decide the cases. As a result of the relentless effort made by the women of Manipur, the Women Movement of 1939 became an eye opener to all sections of people. It gave a clear picture of nationalism in the State. Irabot took the cause of the women's movement of 1939. He was arrested on a charge of sedition under Section 124 of the Indian Penal Code and was sentenced for a term of three years simple imprisonment in connection with the speech which he delivered at the meeting of the Manipur Praja Samiloni at the Police Bazaar on 7th January 1940. After the arrest of H. Irabot Sing people of Manipur became conscious of the issues of that time internally and externally. They have started to work in a more systematic and organized way. The statement of Irabot in the meeting, i.e. (1) The women who bagged for rice had received bayonet points and rifle bullets instead; (2) One handful of rice had been purchased at the price of two handful of blood; (3) Rice export would not have been closed without the spilling of blood; (4) The people should take revenge and remedy the wrong ; and (5) He exhorted the men folk to rise up, not to fear jail and take revenge for the blood of the Brahmini; were exaggerated by different organizations like Manipu Praja Sanmelani, Manipur Krishak Sabha, Manipur Youth League, Manipur Mahila Sangh and Manipur Student Federation. All these organizations worked together for a responsible government of Manipur. After 14th January 1940 it became apparent that the lead had now passed from the women to the men of the Congress group.

Nationalism in Pre-Independence India worked along the lines of selected strategies of resistance which included the appropriation of the popular and the indigenous as "a repository of natural truth, the classification of a timeless tradition, uncontaminated by colonialism and finally, the establishment of the hegemonic domain of nationalism. The first strategy enables subordinated peoples to recoup their indigenous cultural traditions and retrieve their repressed histories. Yet, while doing so, it tends towards the fixity and fetishism of identities. Tradition resonate equality frequently with cultural nationalism. The ideological position opens up a space for defence of the most obscurantist position in the name of cultural nationalism.[54] The hegemonic domain of nationalism, established as a unifying force against imperial domination, holds the greatest threat to women, non-bourgeoisie classes and minority groups in South Asia. It is significant that the vocabulary markings and signifiers of pre-Independence nationalism continue to be enforced in the post-Independence nationalism continues to be enforced in the post-Independence milieu. Political decolonization and the ensuing celebration of freedom, however momentums, do not by themselves inaugurate a new history, but call for a ceaseless endeavour to project a pure identity through myths of origin, whether it is Aryan, Dravidians or Islamic. As a result those people outside the privileged groups became the focus of a denigrator's rhetoric.[55]

Women were put in the forefront at first; but most of them left before anything serious happened. Mr. Gimson asked the judicial members of the Durbar to prepare a detailed and accurate account of the events of 14th January 1940 for submission to His Highness who would publish the statement of what had happened.[56] In a real sense, history shows that Manipuri women have a great role in order to maintain economic stability and social harmony in Manipur.

The two important social movements during the British Imperialism in Manipur, one in 1904, and the other in 1939. were lead by women community of Manipur for the sake of the whole society, in order to maintain economic stability and social harmony. But it is not wrong to say that any spectator became confused when they come to know and see what a Manipuri woman can do when they are in group.

NOTES

1. Saharia Umesh Ch. and Bhattacharjee 'Crime Against Woman, A Problem of Female Emancipation' in Ray B. Dutta and Ray Asok Kumar (ed), *Women Emancipation, Focus North East India,* Om Publications, New Delhi, 2008, p. 112.
2. Amalesh Banergee, Women Eemancipation and Development, N.E Perspectives, in. Ray B. Dutta and Ray Asok Kumar (ed), *Women Emancipation, Focus North East India,* Om Publications, New Delhi, 2008, p. 257.
3. Saifun Nessa, 'Emancipation of Women and Sustainable Social Development' in Ray B. Dutta and Ray Asok Kumar (ed), *Women Emancipation, Focus North East India,* Om Publications, New Delhi, 2008, pp. 115-16.
4. Ghosh Chitra, Ray Soma, Chande Chandni, *Opening the Closed Windows,* Progressive Publishers, Kolkata, 2002, p. 56.
5. *Ibid.,* p. 62.
6. K. A. Kunjakkan, *Feminism and Indian Realities,* Mittal Publication, New Delhi, 2002, p. 209.
7. Roy Ashin, *Violence against Women,* Rajat Publication, New Delhi, 2003, p. 6.
8. *Times of India,* dated.1.2.2009, p. 7.
9. K. A. Kunjakkan, *op. cit.,* p. 89.
10. *Ibid.,* p. 209.
11. Micheal S. Kimmul, *The Gendered Society,* Oxford University Press, New York, 2000, p.XI.
12. Sarkar Tanika, *Hindu Wife, Hindu Nation, Community, Religion and Cultural Nationalism,* Permanent Block, Delhi, 2001, p. 21.
13. Roy Ashin, *op. cit,* p. 5.
14. Sarkar Aanchal, *Gender and Development,* Pragun Publications, New Delhi, 2006, p. 5.

15. *Ibid.*
16. Ghosh Chitra, Ray Soma, Chande Chandni, *Op. Cit*, pp. 64-65.
17. *Ibid.*, pp.75-76.
18. Thorner Alice, Krishnaraj Maithreyi, *Ideals, Images and Real Lives*, Sameeksha Trust, 2000, pp.VI-VII.
19. *Ibid.*, pp. 2-3.
20. *The Times of India,* dated 12-09-2007, p.6.
21. *The Times of India*, dated. 23-08-2007, p.1.
22. Biswas Saswati, 'The Gender Concerns in North East India and Relevance of Social Movements', in Ray Basudeb Dutta and Ray Asok Kumar (ed), *Women Emancipation, Focus North East India,* Om Publication, New Delhi, 2008, pp. 94-95.
23. Ksh. Bimola Devi, Women and Human Rights in Conflict Situation in Manipur, in *Human Rights and Women in North East India,* Women Studies Center, Dibrugarh University, Assam.
24. Th. Binarani Devi, 'Insurgency and Human Rights in Manipur', in Ray Asok Kumar and Dev B.J., (ed) *Terrorism and Human Rights in North East India*, Om Publications, New Delhi, 2007, p. 123.
25. Ksh. Bimola Devi, *op. cit*.
26. Biswas Saswati, *op. cit*. p.99.
27. Parth N. Mukherji, 'Naxalbari Movement and the Peasant Revolt in North Bengal', in M.S.A.Rao (ed) *Social Movements in India,* Manohar Publication, Delhi, 1984, p.18.
28. Sharma R.N. and Sharma R.K., *Political Sociology,* Media Promoters and Publishers Pvt. Ltd., Bombay, 1986, pp. 385-86.
29. L. Ibungohal Sing, *An Introduction to Manipur,* Imphal, 1960, p.31.
30. Ksh. Bimola Devi, 'Manipuri Women: A Study', in N. Sanajaoba Sing (ed). *Manipur: Past and Present,* Mittal Publication, Delhi.
31. N. Ibobi Sing, *Manipur Administration 1709-1907,* N. Ibetombi Devi, 2003 p. 46
32. N. Joykumar Sing, 'First Women Agitation, 1904', in Lal Dena (ed), *History of Manipur,* Orbit Publishers and Distributors, New Delhi, 1990, p.124.
33. Ganguly, J.B., 'The Meitei Women Power', in B. Dutta Ray and Ray Asok Kumar (ed) *Dynamics of Power Relations in Tribal Societies of North East India,* Om Publications, New Delhi, 2006, p.191.
34. K. Manimohan Sing, *Nupilan,* K. Premlata Devi, Imhal, p. 49.

35. *Ibid.*, p.49.
36. N. Joykumar Sing, *op. cit*, p.123.
37. *Ibid.*, p.124.
38. K. Manimohan Sing, *op. cit.*, p. 50.
39. *Ibid.*, p.51
40. Ganguly, J.B, *op. cit*, p.189.
41. K. Manimohan Sing, *op. cit*. pp.106-07.
42. *Ibid*. p.109.
43. N. Joykumar Sing, *op.cit.*, p.147.
44. Ksh. Bimola Devi, 'Women in Social Movements in Manipur', in M.N. Karna (ed), *Social Movements in North East India*, Indus Publishing Company, New Delhi,1998, p.79.
45. K. Manimohan Sing, *op. cit.*, p.171.
46. *Ibid.*, p.170.
47. Zehol, Lucy T.V., 'Women's Movement in Manipur: Some Observations', in M. N.Karna, (ed), *Social Movements in North East India*, Indus Publishing Company, New Delhi, 1998, pp. 69-70.
48. N. Joykumar Sing, *op. cit*, p.148.
49. K. Manimohan Sing, *op. cit*, p.179.
50. *Ibid.*, p.173.
51. *Ibid.*, p.198.
52. *Ibid.*, pp.198-99.
53. N. Joykumar Sing, *op. cit.*, p.148.
54. Silva, Neluka, *The Gendered Nation, Contemporary Writings from South Asia*, Sage Publications, New Delhi, 2004, p.18.
55. *Ibid.*, p.19.
56. K. Manimohan Sing, *op. cit.*, p. 208.

4

Women's Organisation and Women's Movement after the Merger Agreement (1949)

The activities of women and youths in groups as members of voluntary organization, pressure groups have a forceful impact on the political process of the state. After the accession of Manipur to the Union of India, the women community once again energized their role in the struggle for restoration of democracy and fought against the undemocratic Advisory Council (1952-53), the Territorial Council, finally fought for the movement for statehood. With the beginning of 1940s the Manipur Mahila Sanmellani was reconstituted with new college educated girls who returned from Bengal. When Manipur merged to the Indian Union in 1949, it became a Part of the State instead of a full-fledged statehood which was quite contrast to the hope and aspirations of the people in connection with their political status. With the beginning of 1950s the demand for full responsible government became stronger. The people became restless and observed *hartal* all over Manipur. *Bandh* and *hartal* characterized the social and political life of the state. A separate women's conference was held and a Women's Assembly Demand Committee was formed. Consequently, the committee observed "A Women's Assembly Demand Day" on 21st April 1960 at Imphal.

Before 1950s the womenfolk of Manipur organized together a collective force and launched any movement against the authority with any issue which was happened from time to time. After 1950s women have started to work for any movement within the framework of formal organizational structures and sometimes in collaboration with other frontal organizations.

The activities of women are so advanced in all fields now-a-days. Modern Indian Women are objects of administration by people of the rest of the world for the role they played in the country's public life. Women in India have not only reached the highest position of power and equal political and civil rights as men without having to fight for them, but they also have been increasingly joining the higher ranks of administration.

With the beginning of 1980s, the law and order situation of Manipur has become bad to worse condition. The entire valley was under heavy combing operation by the army in order to flush out the 'extremists'. Ever since then, the women in different parts of the state have been organizing themselves against the combing operation and over-reactionary activities of the Army. On April 26, 1980 an armed insurgent group attacked the Central Reserve Police Force, at Patsoi Khunnou Bazar and took away the arms. In retaliation, The Central Reserve Police Force conducted search operation in the area and tortured, harassed the innocent civilian. Women were raped and one woman called Bino, who was hiding with her small son in the paddy store, was killed. The CRPF personnel also killed three more persons. All the people of the area including the women were detained in the sun without any food.[1] After the incident, women from different parts of the state gathered spontaneously in front of the Chief Minister's bungalow and shouted anti-combing slogans followed by demonstrations in the city. This had some amount of desired effect. After the incident women started to guard the locality from the army excesses at night with torch. Now such activities of women group are popularly known as Meira Paibi Movement.

The civil society protest movements organized by the women from time to time against unjust government decisions have impacted on the state policy in respect of human liberty. This may be reckoned as a significant feature of women power in Manipur. They are influencing public opinion in favour of their rights in sharing, inheriting owning movable and immovable properties including land, rights in the political decision making system.

Now-a-days, Manipur the tiny border state of India, *i.e.* witnesses a period of transition marked with day light murders, robberies, lootings, arm snatching, street fighting, ambush, and consequential army operations and alleged tortured on the civil populace. There is not a day, for a considerable span of time in the recent past, the front pages of the national papers or local papers missed reports on such ugly scenario, which simply made the law enforcing authorities a force. The whole functionary of the state was sometimes seemed to have been paralyzed, people were always panic stricken. The crimes were also committed even in the very centre of the city and security zones, at the very noise of the police. Indeed, what was imagined as the worst occurred as a regular phenomenon in Manipur resulting into confused state of affairs? At this juncture, the women organizations along with other organizations and NGOs have been contributing a great role in the normalization of such situations.

Although women's organizations are particularly strong in Manipur and have traditionally played a leading role in initiating peace in the region, there is hardly an organization that cuts across the narrow ethnic lines separating their members. It is true that the predominantly Meitei rage against any attempt to vivisect Manipur was never translated into any mass pogromme directed against even the minority of the Nagas living in the Imphal valley; but there is reportedly no communication between them either. Indifference after all is not hostility.

It is important to point out the limitations of a peripherally located movement.

1. The movement does not get adequate courage from the national media. As a result, the managers of state can shield their accountability.
2. The ripple effect being minimum of a peripheral movement, it hardly affects the life of 'other' people elsewhere. Had Nagaland, or Assam, or Manipur, or Tripura been located somewhere in the mainland, like Jharkhand, the Indian state would have walked extra miles to address their grievances. Since a movement in the region does not affect life in the mainland, a policy of 'get boil in your own steam' is possible to adopt.
3. As the state, instead of addressing the core issues, adopts some sort of delaying tactics, the movement recurs time and again in different forms.
4. As it exhausts the tools of democratic protest, violence becomes an inevitable option that represents the deep sense of frustration permeating the social psyche.

In connection with the agitation and demonstration of women in Manipur, in the editorial of *Economic and Political Weekly* of 24 July 2004, mentioned: "On the morning of July 15 (2004) they shed their cloths before the headquarters of Assam Rifles in the heart of Imphal holding a banner which proclaimed: 'Indian Army Rape us, Indian Army Take Our Flesh' has been predictably dismissed by the army authorities as part of a pattern of such protests that take place whenever a fresh notification is due to extend the life of the Armed Forces Special Power Act (AFSPA)".[2]

Demanding repeal of the Armed Forces Special Power Act, 1958, Irom Sharmila Chanu, a resident of Imphal East District, Kongpal Kongkham Leikai, has been on a fast-unto-death agitation since a day after Assam Rifles Jawans killed ten civilians at Malom, Imphal West District on November 1, 2000, after an attack of the Assam Rifles by unidentified armed persons. Different agencies, forums etc. echoed with the demand of the Gwangju Awardee Sharmila Chanu and Meira Paibi groups. Not only from the state of Manipur, it was reacted from different states of India and abroad. For all those demanding repeal of the Armed Forces Special Power Act (AFSPA) in Manipur, here is a piece of encouragement from down South. Thousands of people including women activists and filmmakers, from Kerala have requested Defence Minister A.K. Anthony to scrap the controversial Act. Members of the Kerala Coastal Women's Forum conducted a campaign in protest against the Military Act and collected signatures of over 10,000 people. Forum leaders also submitted a petition to A.K. Anthony on Sunday demanding immediate scrapping of AFSPA.[3] In today's insurgency affected Manipur "the Meira Paibi" (women torch bearer—night vigil group of women in Manipur) hold marshals and keep a watch in the neighbourhood where local youths are sometimes forcibly taken by armed personels, both state and non-state forces, arrested and killed and giving charges of different crimes after killing. Sometimes it is confused who had killed—state forces or non-state forces, they are charging each other.

In Manipur, violation of Human Rights coupled with gendered violence. Gender-based violence encompasses a wide range of human rights violation, including sexual abuse of children, rape, domestic violence, sexual assault and harassment, trafficking of women and girls and several harmful traditional practices. Anyone of these abuses can leave deep psychological scars, damage the health of women and girls in general, including their reproductive and sexual health, and in some instances, result in death. Violence against women has been recognized as 'the most pervasive yet least recognized human rights abuse in the world.' Accordingly, the Vienna Human Rights Conference and the Fourth World Conference on Women gave priority to this issue which jeopardizes women's lives, bodies, psychological integrity and freedom. Violence against women and girls constitute the single most prevalent and universal violation of human rights. The United Nations, in keeping with the spirit of the UN Declaration of Human Rights, work in many ways to eliminate this morally unacceptable scourge. UN Conference on Human Rights, the 1979 Convention on the Elimination of All Forms of Discrimination Against Women (CEDAW), the Beijing Declaration, the United Nations Development Fund for Women (UNIFEM) etc. are some of the instruments that would address the issue of gendered violence. Despite regard for the principle of non-discrimination in the enjoyment of rights contained in the UDHR, ICCPR, ICESCR, and other human rights instruments, women were not treated equally at the global level.[4] CEDAW acknowledged that discrimination against women violates the principles of equality of rights and respect for human dignity, and is an obstacle to the participation of women, on equal terms with men, in the political, social, economic and cultural life of their countries. This in turn, affects the development of family and society as a whole. In the armed conflict situation in Manipur many people are killed and kidnapped. Many newly married and unmarried women are forced to commit suicide to save themselves against rape and social abuse by the security forces. With the increase of state violence in the state particularly against the youths and women, the women community in Manipur staged unrobed protest march against custodial rape and killing of Ms. Manorama by the Assam Rifles personnel on 11th July 2004. The demonstrators carried the honour of their community on their bodies and demonstrated that by raping them the army would defile the entire community.[5]

With the main aim of the overall development of the whole society, especially for the improvement of the socio-economic conditions different women organizations are developed in the length and breadth of Manipur. Sometimes strenuous efforts are being made to enforce prohibition, sale of liquor, prostitution, practice of polygamy and welfare programme for women and children.

All Manipur Nupi Marup

This organization is one of the oldest women organizations in Manipur, which have been working as a pressure group with the main objectives of independent indigenous communities should exist harmoniously without any differentiation of caste, colour, race, sex, business etc.[6] Before independence of India and before merging of Manipur to the Indian Union, the name of this organization was 'Manipur Mahella Sanmellani' and the members of this organization took part in the Second Nupilan (Women's movement) of 1939. During that time the Meitei women were not so politically oriented and not highly educated. But they fought against the administrators of that time. At the beginning, the movement directly related with the irregularities and malpractices in the administration of the state. But it gave a right direction for the larger movement against the British for an independent Manipur. While Manipur became a part of the Indian Union in 1949, the expectations of Manipuris from the Government of India was quite contradictory. So, different forms of movements have developed in Manipur. Mahella Sanmellani also joined in those movements including the movement for a full-fledged statehood of Manipur. Some women members were arrested when they made slogans for the statehood of Manipur when Smt. Indira

Gandhi came to Manipur after that incident; Manipur became a full-fledged state from a Union Territory. Just before the arrival of Indira Gandhi, the then Prime Minister of India, member of the Manipur Mahella Sanmellani held a meeting at Waheng Leikai. In that meeting the Manipur Mahella Sanmellani turned into All Manipur Nupi Marup with a formal organizational structure and a constitution of its own on which all the activities of the organization will depend upon. When Manipur became a full-fledged state of Indian Union, the socio-economic and political conditions of the state were not so good. All Manipur Nupi Marup as an independent, non-governmental organization took up different issues. They give pressure to the government from time to time in connection with the socio-economic and political development of the whole society. They are not giving pressure to the government only but also to those groups who are committing crimes like extortion, killing, making damages to the vehicles and vehicle peoples like drivers and vehicle owners, demanding huge ransoms etc.

According to the opinion of the All Manipur Nupi Marup, if Manipur is a part of the Indian Union, she will get all facilities and recognitions under the provisions of the Indian Constitution and the laws of the country. She is represented by only two representatives in the Lok Sabha and only one representative in the Rajya Sabha. While Manipur became a part of the Indian Union, Manipuri language was not included in the Eighth Schedule of the Indian Constitution. Movements were there from different directions—students' organizations, clubs, women's organizations, workers or employees unions etc. All Manipur Nupi Marup joined in these movements. The movement for the inclusion of Manipuri language in the Eighth Schedule of the Indian Constitution became so serious during 1980s. They submitted memorandums, called bandhs, sit in protest, strike in different parts of Manipur and Delhi also. The Government of India was unable to remain in deaf ear. Three languages,

Manipuri, Nepali, and Konkani were announced as included in the Eighth Schedule of the Indian Constitution on 20th August 1992.

The All Manipur Women Nupi Marup realized that if and when women members are involved in the decision-making process, then they will understand about the feelings, conditions, and situations clearly for the society as a whole and for women specifically. For instance, in the Manipur State Legistative Assembly, at present, out of the total membership of 60 there is only one women MLA. Even she has no voice in the House. So this organization in support of the women seats reservation in the state legislative assemblies and Parliament held rally and sit in protest in front of the Parliament on 3rd December 1997, submitted memorandums to the Parliament of India.

Even though the United Nations Organization announced the Universal Declaration of Human Rights on 10th December 1948, societies are still far away from enjoying those rights. Manipur is not an exception but more serious, so the proclaimed rights are to be reclaimed for the ruling authorities to enforce and implement. Violence is a political issue and it is relevant to all. Both men and women are victims of violence in Manipur. In the name of the maintenance of law and order different Acts and Bills are using by the authority. With these Acts and Bills a number of innocent people have lost their lives. In connection with any socio-political and economic problem civil society organizations launched movements. Instead of quick implementation of the demands, the authority imposes curfew and used huge paramilitary forces for controlling the movement with violent actions. The All Manipur Nupi Marup took into account in such activities of the government and tried to protect the basic minimum rights of the people, i.e. the right to life. In different occasions like the killing of the people, raping of women and looting of properties in the name of search operations like, incidence of Patsoi in April 1980, killing of innocent people at the volleyball ground at Heirangoithong, killing of 18 innocent people in June 2001 in connection with the extension of Indo-Naga cease fire without any territorial limits, killing of 11 persons by the security forces from 26 February to 10 March 2004, killing of K. Rishikanta of Kakwa in November 2009, kidnapping and killing of the innocent persons like Manoj Kumar Sethi, L. Elizabeth etc. the All Manipur Nupi Marup launched different movements and the government also could not remained in silent. Violation of human rights is occurring in different directions. One form of right is violated; it is followed by a chain of human rights violations. When Dr. Thingnam Kishan Sing, SDO was kidnapped on 13th February 2009 along with his five other staffs and found his death body along with the death bodies of two other staffs on 18th February 2009 in a brutal manner. People became scare off when they see the condition of the death bodies. Bandhs were called in different parts by different communities in different areas of Manipur from 18th to 20th February 2009. In the name of controlling the movement and for avoiding the unwanted occurrences, Sri O. Ibobi Sing declared curfew through the respective D.Cs in Manipur. People were not allowed to organize any rally, demonstrations and even people were not allowed to go and share with the bereaved family. Civil police and army used rubber bullets, tear gases etc., for dispersing the public.

As a result of these activities, people suffered minor and major injuries. Even younger brother of Dr. Kishan was injured from rubber bullet of the police on 19th February evening. During the curfew people were not allowed to go out and even pharmacies were closed down. So, one case of violation of human rights created a chain of human rights violation. So the All Manipur Nupi Marup and civil society organizations demanded to find out the real criminal(s) and to take up necessary actions and to remove curfew. Extortion by militant is rampant in Manipur and Chidambaram wanted to put an end to it. Government officials are regularly being threatened by rebels not meeting their extortion demands. Many a times, funds meant for development are siphoned off to militant. In different occasions, public and civil society organizations are saying that Manipur Government is neglecting hilly areas. As a consequent step, they are doing anything against the Government directly and indirectly to the masses. They set ablaze the government buildings, educational institutions, called bandhs and blockades etc. True colour of the underground organizations towards the welfare activities of the government have started to show after Union Home Minister P. Chidambaram's instruction to go all out to stop extortion by militants. During his February 3rd, 2009 visit to Imphal, the Union Home Minister asked the government to stop extortion by rebels which was hampering development. After that, the state government instructed officials to ensure that funds meant for development don't lend in the hands of militants. Sri P. K. Jha, the SDO of Tadubi in Senapati District, has come under rebel's threat. Superintendent of Police (Senapati) Nishit Kumar Ujwal said a complaint was received by his office and the district administration that four or five armed cadres of Federal Government of Nagaland (FGN) had demanded Rs. 1 (one) lakh from Jha and threatened him with dire consequences if he refused to do so. SDO Kasom Khullen, Sri Th. Kishan Sing has opposed militants attempt to take away the funds sanctioned under the National Rural Employment Guarantee Scheme (NREGS) for Ukhrul District. Official sources said it was NSCN (IM) cadres who had abducted the officer.[7] NSCN (IM) announced that Dr. Th. Kishan Sing and his two staffs were killed under the guidelines of Lt. Colonel H. Ningsen, Commanding Officer Kuisumang batallian.[8]

Violence against women exists in various forms in everyday life in all societies. There are several instances where rape victims in any society do not report the atrocity committed against them for fear of physical safety. This speaks poorly of both—which is deeply patriarchal in its attitudes—and our law-enforcing machinery. Instead of enabling women who have been victims of sexual assault cope with their trauma, large sections of our society often heap indignity on them. Delhi is by far the most unsafe city for women in this country. But it is not just here that women are vulnerable of crime, especially of the sexual sort. The National Crime Records Bureau, in its report for 2007, documents that there were 513 reported rape cases in Delhi City. This was way above the number of cases reported in Mumbai, which stood at 171, Bangalore reported 62 cases, Indore 74, Pune 65 and Chennai 46. And this is just a count of those cases that were reported.[9] In Manipur different incidents occurred in connection with the violation of women's right like kidnapping, raping, killing, cases like, Neelam Panchavaya, Tamphasana, Ahanjaobi, L. Elizabeth etc. In such above cases The All Manipur Nupi Marup directly involved in the protest movement for finding out the real culprit, to give reasonable punishment and gave moral and physical support to those families. India aspires to great power status. It provides itself on an impressive economy growth record and increasing international clout. This is perhaps justified given facts about the overall performance of our economy, especially when compared to that of other countries in this time of global economic gloom. However, India's progress is, and will continue to be, severely stymied if it does not secure the life, security and dignity of one half of its population. No matter how rapidly its economic grows, its prestige will not improve much if its women continue to be treated with scant respects. One important activities of the organization is in connection with any case of human rights violation case it should not be compromise with *ex-gratia*. Their claim is not only to the armed personnels of the government, who are using power but to any other forum for not to violate the basic minimum rights of the people.

Powerful governments and armed groups are deliberately fomenting fear to erode human rights and to create an increasingly polarized and dangerous world. We need today a substantive and long-term investment in human rights, to build effective systems of justice and accountability to strengthen the human rights machinery and to protect the rights of women. There should be respect for human rights defenders and for economic, social as well as civil and political rights of the poor and marginal communities. Armed groups fixed their muscles and engaged in massive abuse of human rights and international humanitarian law. In the name of revolutionary or something else, any armed groups violated the rights of the people in the state. They are demanding huge amount of money in the name of donation. Manipur is connected with other parts of the country by two national highways only. i.e. National Highway No. 39 and 53. These two national highways are becoming the gamble of outlawed armed tribal groups, and a number of civil societies and tribal student's organizations with different demands from time to time. They have burned down the buses and trucks; looted properties and money, killed passengers and drivers; raped and molested women including minors etc. In connection with such activities, the All Manipur Nupi Marup, on 2nd May 2007 organized meetings and conferences at Moreh Bazar, Tengnoupal Bazar and Pallel Bazar along with the women of those areas. They have discussed about what are the problems faced by the people altogether and how to remove all such problems and how to get a normal and peaceful life by performing their activities. After that, on 21st May 2007, they organized a rally at Imphal. That rally was participated by the women from different parts of the state in a peaceful democratic way. They appealed to stop such type of atrocity or inhuman attitude. Their plan was not confined only to Imphal but proposed such type of peace process to different towns of the state like, Sekmai Bazar, Kangpokpi Bazar, Noneh Bazar, Jiri Bazar, Bishnupur Bazar, Moirang Bazar, Churachandpur Bazar, Kumbi Bazar.[10]

In this modern globalized world, the activities and

positions of the women are necessary to take into account minutely. What are the problems faced by the women, the activities they are performing within their social norms, their involvement in this modern scientific liberal outlook etc. are need to examine and to take up steps for strengthening their positions with proper legislation. If there is proportionate number of women in the legislative bodies, i.e. state legislative assemblies and parliament, the issues and problems of women can acknowledge in an easy way. So, there is an urge for a 3 per cent seat reservation for the women in the legislative bodies with the beginning of 1990s. In this movement, the most popular women organizations of India like the All India Democratic Women's Association, Center for Women's Development Studies, Joint Women's Programme, Mahella Dafta Samittee, National Federation of Indian Women, All India Women Conference etc. are taking great role. The All Manipur Nupi Marup also joined the movement at the state and national level. They mobilized the women of the state to take part in the protest movement (*Dharna*) of 3rd December 1997 in front of the Parliament, during its winter session. Still they are taking part in the movement.

Manipur is just tiny border state where the different indigenous ethnic groups are living together. There is a great need for the unity and integrity of all the people of this state. So they took part in all the movements organized by other organization like rally, sit in protest etc. and they also organized different rallies in this matter. In 2001 June, while the Indo-NSCN (IM) talk was held at Bangkok which make a threat to the territorial limit of Manipur. The All Manipur Nupi Marup prepared a draft memorandum for submission to the Governor of Manipur at about 9 a.m. of June 18. But the government announced curfew and the incidence for killing of 14 innocent people in a single day was occurred. After this incident "Struggle Committee on withdrawal of Cease Fire" was formed by different civil society organizations. The

All Manipur Nupi Marup took a leading role in the formation of this Committeé. They submitted a memorandum to the Prime Minister of India for not to extend the Indo-NSCN (IM) cease fire towards the territorial jurisdiction of Manipur.[11] The Government of India also reviewed their order, i.e. the term 'without territorial limit' was deleted.

Kha Nongpok Apunba Nupi Lup

Kha Nongpok Apunba Nupi Lup was established in 1993, by the women of Prem Nagar, Chingdong Leikai, Heinou Makhong, Khunnou and Bazar Leikai. Even though the Lup has no proper constitution of its own, with the great initiative of Smt Kh. Keinya Leima as the founder President, they have been trying to perform all the socio-economic activities which can enhance the position of women in the area and to bring a peaceful society as a whole. As Moreh is such an area which is targeted by the businessmen of all communities the socio-economic problems of the area, especially for the women is vulnerable. Women from different parts of the state and from other states of India and even from neighbouring countries come here and they are trying to get the means of their livelihood. Main business activities, i.e. buying to carrying goods for others' goods are doing by the women. On the way, i.e. Imphal to Moreh, we can find different army, customs and police check posts. By taking chance of stopping the vehicles in the check posts, women are selling eatable goods along with the locally available goods to the travellers. Women are becoming the victims of unwanted activities like black marketeers (carrying of drugs, alcohols, Heroin No.4 etc., which are not allowed by the law of the country), sex workers etc. And sometime they are becoming the victims of rape, molestation, human traffickers, gender crimes etc. Kha Nongpok Aunba Nupi Lup, in collaboration with other frontal organizations and association tried to remove such problems in the area especially and involved such type of issues which are happening in any part of the state. Lam Khulling Mate, a physically challenged women, who is struggling her life with a small *pan* shop of Moreh was raped and killed by knotting her neck by her own *chunni* (cloth) on the night of 22nd January 2009 by Ipham Aamir Khan and Achom Romen. Before finding out the real culprit, bandh was called by Kha Nongpok Apunba Nupi Lup along with other organizations and submitted memorandum to the Government for finding out the real culprit and punishment. The agony of the Lup reached the heart of the underground organizations. So UNLF, PLA, KYKL etc. jointly tried to find out the real culprits and the said duo were found but and given death punishment. Before killing them, the UGs called a press meet and the duo were also admitted their crimes and narrated the story how Miss Mate was raped and killed. For avoiding such crime against women furthermore by any person, death punishment was given to the real culprit even though that was against the law of the country.

With the main aim of economic empowerment and to give a way for earning their livelihood the association formed Moreh Handloom and Silk Weavers Co-operative Society. After the formation of this co-operative society, weavers training programmes were held (two-batches of 25 trainees). For running co-operative society, they have demanded some financial help or assistance from the government of Manipur. The Government of Manipur has given some financial assistance, but that could not meet the needs for the infrastructure and beginning of the work of the society.

As a frontal organization of the area, the Kha Nongpok Apunba Nupi Lup look after all or interfere all the socio-economic activities of the area mainly—Prem Nagar, Ward No.4, Chingdong Leikai, Heinou Makhong, Khunou, Bazar Leikai. Meira paibi groups are also formed for emergency and minute actions of the mentioned specific areas.

By taking chance of the location, i.e. the transit point for the foreign countries, the people of the area suffered the problems of armed conflict situation. As a result of this armed conflict situation, people are facing the problems of insurgency problems. The Lup is blaming the situation to the Government of India, especially by the armed personnels created such a lot of problems.[12]

Throwing of bombs, attack to the state forces, snatching of arms, putting of bombs, bomb blast in the public places etc. by the unidentified armed groups is becoming so common in Manipur. In the name of searching of those armed groups the state forces do anything whatever they like. No one can say anything against the activities of both the state and non-state forces. But such situations disturbed the normal life and security of the civil populace. So, The Kha Nongpok Apunba Nupi Lup staged a Dharna (sit in Protest) on 23rd April 2009 at Moreh along with other organizations and local people in connection with throwing of bomb to the 31st Assam Rifles Post near Moreh Gate No. 2 which is one of the most crowded area of Moreh Town. They have demanded not to creat any situation which will disturb peace, security and normal life of the people from any side.[13]

Not only in the area, the Lup have joined in almost all the social movements of Manipur spontaneously like the formation of Apunba Lup, during the time of custodial rape and killing of Thanjam Manorama Devi by the Army. They are giving pressure to the government for settling all the disputes with proper judgment by giving punishment to those real culprits. On the night of 26th February 2009 they organized a torch rally at the Moreh area in connection with the merciless killing of SDO Kashom Khullen, Dr. Th. Kishan Sing along with his two staffs by the NSCN (IM). They hold the placards like handover the real culprit to the government of Manipur, take a criminal case over the Deputy Commissioner of Ukhrul etc.

Moreh is a small border town of Chandel District. Indian

government, through the DoNER Ministry has been giving special interest in connection with the development of this area. But the local people are facing financial problems, basic minimum needs of their livelihood etc. So the Kha Nongpok Apunba Nupi Lup demanded proper implementation of Public Distribution System in the area. As a response, Food and Civil Supply Minister, Sri Y. Irabot Sing came to Moreh and meets with the women groups and gave assurance for proper implementation of Public Distribution System. On the spot also Sri Irabot supplied kerosene oil and sugar.

All Manipur Social Reformation and Development Samaj

The All Manipur Social Reformation and Development Samaj was established in 1974-75 and it became a registered body in 1977-78 (Reg. No. 2441). The main aims and objectives of this association are to serve for the welfare of women community, used its rights as well as to control and total prohibition of drugs and alcohol in the society. This association will work to all nook and corner of the state and there will be no difference between caste, creed and community. It is a non-political body. The main activities of this association are fighting with the social evils, e.g. drunkards, drug addicts, rapists, murderers, communal or ethnic conflicts etc. For giving awareness and sensitization to the rural areas they organized seminars, conferences, meetings etc.[14]

The activities of the civil society organizations are not an end in itself. It is a means to an end. They can perform only the input function in the political process. If their activities are not responded by the government, they shattered off. In such situations the All Manipur Social Reformation and Development Samaj does not remain in silent hopelessly. They knocked even the door of the head of the State

Legislature and Executive in a formal way. During a short period of 1975-87, the association handed over 342 cases of drunkards to the local police. They are of the opinion that maximum crimes in Manipur are happening as a result of the using alcohol and drugs by the men folk. After using alcohol and drugs, they committed a lot of violent actions to the family members, especially to their wives and children. If they have no money for buying alcohol and drugs they asked to their wife and children or to their parents by the unmarried youths. If they are not getting up to these conditions they tried to steel household properties like jewellers. With the influence of alcohol and drugs they commit any crimes, fighting among themselves. So, simply maximum social crimes are happening with influence of drugs and alcohols. So, the association took up the task of Nasha Bandi means to stop drugs and alcohols. But those drunkards who were handed over to the local police were released without taking any action as the discretion of higher ups. In this regard the All Manipur Social Reformation and Development Samaj requested to the then Governor and Ministers of the State. A separate Memo has also been submitted to the then Prime Minister of India on 11th April 1987, requesting him to give special instruction to the police personnels. Subsequent memos of implementing total "Prohibition" have also been submitted to the Chief Minister of Manipur repeatedly— 4th August 1980, 27th August 1980, and 11th August 1984. These were only submission of 'memos' and request. But the existing government remained in a deaf ear. So, the association decided to start a movement with different forms of pressures. On 31st March 1990, the association submitted a memo again to the Governor and the Chief Minister separately, but no response positively. Consequently, on 13th September 1990, they smashed 39 cases of IMFL in the Imphal Bazar and gheraoed many foreign liquor shops, Government may collect taxes but what are the social problems which are happening after having alcohol, the association things need to take into account. As a result of the demand and pressure of the association, the Manipur State Legislative Assembly has introduced the bill of 'Prohibition' in 1991. Social problems created by drunkards have crossed over the limits in certain cases. Sri Khundrakpam Shyamkisor Sing of Khurai Ahongei killed his wife Khundrakpam (ongbi) Sanahanbi Devi on 8-4-93. All the women sections of Manipur soaked the incidents and protested from all directions. In this case also, the All Manipur Social Reformation and Development Samaj took a leading role and the culprit was arrested and put into jail. A campaign for safeguarding and killing of innocent women was launched and demanded the action against the real culprit by the women of Manipur under the leadership of All Manipur Social Reformation and Development Samaj. They submitted a memorandum to the Chief Minister of Manipur on 11th April 1993. Another heart felt incidents was occurred in connection with the use of drug was happened in 1987 in Manipur. An innocent five years small boy was killed on 24th April 1987 by two drug addicts for just a small earring worth Rs. 180 only. For this merciless killing, the association organized meetings, processions, to draw public sentiments and also pursuing the government to punish the wrong doers.

When a person is influenced by drugs or alcohols, it affects not only to him and his family, but to all the environments. At present AIDS/HIV infected persons are increasing at an alarming rate in Manipur. So, the association organized seminars, conventions and giving awareness to the women of all over the state in collaboration with the local bodies. They made a slogan to root out the social evils.

There are a number of gender crimes, rape cases, molestation, killing etc. in the state. On 24-1-1986, Miss Luingamla Muinao of Ukhrul District was mercilessly murdered by two army personnels and again on 8-3-1986, Km. Neelam Panchabhaiya discovered dead half floating in the Imphal River in a suspicious manner. People raised hue and cry throughout the state. The All Manipur Social Reformation and Development Samaj took a leading role along with other frontal organizations like AMSU, MSF etc. They submitted a memorandum to the Hon'ble Prime Minister on 18-3-1986. They have requested to look into the matter and requested to punish the alleged two army personnel mentioned in the memo and demanded a judicial enquiry into the case of Neelam Panchabhaya, to bring out the real culprits. Raped and mercilessly killing of Km. Kunjarani Devi and Km. R. K. Tamphasana Devi make a great soak to the motherly feelings of the association. On 24-2-1992, one tribal widow, named Lalmalsomi, 35 years, of Kom community, who have four children was captured by some Anti-Social Gang Groups. Her case was taken up by the association with the help of State Police forces and saved the life of innocent widow in time. The Gang Party was also arrested.[15]

The association is fighting with the atrocities of the Armed Personnel with different Acts and Bills in the state of Manipur. The world famous naked protest in front of the Assam Rifles Forces in July 2004 was a remarkable protest performed by the women of All Manipur Social Reformation and Development Samaj. On 10th December 2008, under the leadership of Smt. K. Taruni Devi, President of the association formed agroup called 'Sharmila Kanba Lup' at PDA Complex Porompat. Their motto is to support Sharmila and demand to remove AFSPA from Manipur. A continuous relay hunger strike is still going on from different parts of the state.[16] People, mainly women of all sections support this movement because the cases related with the violation of human right is increasing so much, and Army and state forces commit the crime of human right violation in the name of this Act.

Manipur Univercity Working Women's Association

Women are working by forming different associations or

organizations as a pressure group in Manipur. Their area of activities as a pressure group has no limit. They are involving in all areas like removal of social evils, economic problems, political drawbacks or backwardness etc. For the removal of all such problems we need to understand—what are the rooms, where the women can intrude into, how to remove the problems etc. The surest means for the above mentioned issues is the education of the people. With the help of academic knowledge women can understand as to what are the facilities which women can get, and what are things which they need to do, within the framework of the state and central government and facilities provided by the international agencies and forums. It will make a bridge between the civil society and the decision makers. So the working ladies of Manipur University formed an association called the Manipur University Working Women's Association in 1992. It was formed with the great initiative of Prof. Ksh. Bimola Devi, former Dean, School of Social Sciences, Manipur University, as its founder President. The main aims and objectives of the association are women's academic empowerment, gender awareness, academic interference of day to day happenings etc.[17] For achieving their aims and objectives, they are organizing talk programme, interaction programme, seminars, conferences etc. periodically. They also published a journal called '*Woman*'.[18]

All the regular lady staffs, both teaching and non-teaching staffs are the members of this association. For running the association and organizing programme, all the members contributed Rs. 10 per month.[19]

Ushoipokpi Tharourok Women Development Association, Ushoipokpi, Lilong

There is a widespread perception that Muslim women are among the most backward, illiterate and oppressed group in the world. In the media they are always shown clad in *burqa* or wrapped in *Hijab* (viel). Meanwhile the Muslim women are on the move in various Muslim countries. In every country or countries where considerable Muslim populations are there like India, education is spreading fast among the Muslim women. This certainly brings increased awareness among the women themselves and they press for their rights, both Islamic and Secular. In Manipur, Muslim women are assimilated with local majority women, i.e. Meitei women. They also formed different organizations and associations voluntarily and worked for the benefit of the society. They worked for the safeguard and upliftment of Muslim women, removal of social evils, and development of the whole society as well. The Ushoipokpi Tharourok Women Development Association, Ushoipokpi, Lilong is such an association. It was established in 2000.[20]

This organization strongly condemned the torture and violence against women and girl child. In Manipur, the cases of torture of women and girl child by their opposite sex and even by their family members are increasing day by day. Especially in the Muslim society, this organization took up different cases and they submitted memorandum to the government. They are trying to solve all the problems with the help of state police forces.

A woman from Nungei Khunnou got Nikah and left her by her husband. After five years, in 2004, the association took up the case as requested by the victim women. With the support of Lilong Police Station, the association caught the accused husband and gave compensation to the victim woman. They also instructed the guy not to commit such mistake further more. Such types of crimes are common to the Muslim populated areas of Manipur. As another case, on 1st May 2004, one girl was eloped by an IRB personnel and stays one night with him and left the girl. When the matter came to the office of the association, they called out all the women from the area and went to the Lilong Police

Station. They lodged complain regarding the matter but the response of the Officer-in-Charge was not satisfactory to those women who came to complain about the matter. They again submitted an application about the said matter to the DGP of Manipur. Consequently, the Officer-in-Charge took up the case in a smooth progress conditionally.

In Manipur, maximum vegetables and eggs in the market are coming from Lilong area. But in 2002 there was a serious flood in the state. That affected Lilong area so bitterly. People have lost their house, animals, birds etc. Crop was failed for the said year. The help and relief facilities were only on the local papers and media channels. During that time, the association gave serious pressure to the Government of Manipur for help and even seeds which they can sow for beginning through the concerned agriculture department.

Women in the Muslim society are not only confined to the household and economic activities, they took part in all the social movement of Manipur which are happening from time to time. There was a big rally jointly organized by AMKIL and NIPCO on September 28, 2000. The members of the association mobilized the local women about the social issue and joined the mass rally. Not only this incident had they joined in all the mass movements like removal of AFSPA, Nasha Bandi etc.

Kuki women are one of the most socially handicapped groups among the different women groups of different tribal communities in Manipur. But their activities, at present are not confining within the socio-economic front of the domestic affairs. They also formed groups and organizations in a formal manner and give pressure to the government with different demands in a democratic way. Not only those specific demands raised by themselves they also joined and support in all the socio-economic movements which are launched by any group of any community. Some important Kuki women organizations are—Kuki Women's Human Right Network, Kuki Mothers Association, Kuki Women's Union Manipur etc.

The Kukis Women Human Right Network

Traditionally the Kuki women were not socially aware. They are very simple, innocent and hard working. From down to sunset they are working in the forest and agricultural field with singing and dancing. Coming back to their home they get their meal with their family members, they started the work of embroidery, weaving, etc. With the advent of Christanity and after getting adjustment with this changing process of the society and education, the Kuki women started to take part in the movement which is reacted over the social, economic and political issues of the society from time to time.

As a reaction to the various Anti-state and Anti-Manipuri activities which directly threatened to the territorial integrity of Manipur different youths and students organizations including women organization took up different steps. Actually the people of Manipur realize the imperative need of strengthening the emotional social bonds of all indigenous people of Manipur even stronger by respecting and protecting each others economic, social and cultural rights and by realizing the shared common destiny as one people with one political aspiration which shall never be compromise. In all the activities of the people of Manipur for this purpose, the Kuki women are not remained silent. The Kuki Women Human Right Network Manipur condemned the uncivilized act of the security forces in firing upon anti-cease fire protestors on June 18, 2001, resulting in the death of 18 innocent people. For protection of the territorial integrity of Manipur the Organizing Committee of Territorial Integrity of Manipur (OCTIM) organized a mass rally on August 4, 1997. The rally was one of the greatest in the history of Manipur in which people from all over state came in large numbers and participated. The security forces could not control the coming in huge numbers and the state administration was paralyzed momentarily. However in keeping up the best tradition of communal harmony no untoward events had been occurred. Another second integrity rally was jointly organized by AMKIL (Apunba Manipur Kanba Ima Lup) and NIPCO (National Identity Protection Committee) on 28th September, 2000. At the end of the meeting comprising all the ethnic groups of Manipur was held at Imphal Pologround and avowed to protect the territorial integrity of Manipur. In both the rallies, the members of the KWHRN with others spontaneously came out in their own traditional dress and shouted the slogan for the protection of the territorial integrity of Manipur.

As the KWHRN was established to protect the rights as well as the atrocities of the army, they involved in any movement called by any sections like Meira paibis, Students organizations etc. During the International Human Rights Conference, Kathmandu, June 2001, Kim Gangte, the General Secretary of the KWHRN expressed her strong opinion to protect basic rights of the people. She stated that if one community try to safeguard their own rights, they must have to think about rights of others and for safeguarding their rights if they violates other's right, they really violates human rights[21].

Kuki Mother's Association

Kuki Mother's Association was established in 1995, with a motto to unite and serve. Rose Mangsi Haokip is its founder President. This association has been working for the unity and integrity of Manipur and trying to remove the social evils. In response to the various anti-state anti-Manipuri activities which directly and indirectly threatened to the territorial integrity of Manipur, the association contributed their share in solving all problems.[22]

Kuki Women's Union, Manipur

This union is working for the protection of human rights,

environmental deterioration, social degradation etc. in Manipur. They are working with the interest of the whole communities who are belonging in different parts of the state.

The excessive activities of the state government and paramilitary forces are becoming the common headlines of the daily newspapers in the state. People were arrested and killed and exhibited pistols, guns, electronic equipments etc. People became scared off such attitude of the armed personnel in Manipur.

On 13-7-2008 one J.A.C. was formed with Smt. Rose Mangshi Haokip, President, Kuki Women's Union, Manipur as the Chairperson in connection with the killing of Thangtinsein Kipgen, student of LL.B. Second Year, and Limbert Len, a player of Kuki Sporting Club were arrested from Sanjembam, under Lamlai Police Station and found their death bodies on 11-7-2008 and they were given charges of involvement in the underground organizations. Different women organizations of different communities, mainly the Meitei communities launched sit-in-protest at New Lambuland junction on 13-7-2008.[23] The main objectives of the movement were :

1. To stop atrocities of Commandos or State actors in the name of counter insurgency in Manipur immediately .
2. To protect human rights.

The demands made by the J.A.C. were :

1. Judicial enquiry to probe extra-judicial killing.
2. Suspension or dismissal of the Police Commandos who were involved in the killing.

The mode of movement was peaceful and democratic

way. No violent action was committed by the movement. It was supported by different frontal organizations as the movement was a reasonable and right step for the present conflict situations of Manipur.

Under the leadership of Kuki Women's Union, at least 100 women staged a demonstration against quarrying on the banks of Imphal River near Kuki Veng on 6-1-2008. It is opposite to the heavily guarded VIP quarters at Babupara. The approach road leading to Haokip Veng and Mahabali has been breached and encroached upon due to the continuous excavation on the river bank.[24]

In politics and other social affairs, women have been able to influence men in many ways directly or indirectly through the village councillor or at least through their husband. In the bygone days when head-hunting was practiced, women played a vital role in saving the lives of men. A woman of the village, during inter-village feuds and wars, would act as an ambassador, and a mediator. In such a case both the warring villages would recognize diplomatic women. The neutral lady-Phukhareila among the Tangkhul, could boldly enter a battle field and intervened between warring groups. She had the right of her own to intervene in the political and social affairs of the society; it is interfered with the general public.[25]

With the passage of time the way of practices may be changed but the women in Tangkhul society still preserving their culture and traditions. The NSCN (IM) and the Assam Rifles developed a situation of tension at Siroy Village of Ukhrul District. The NSCN(IM) signed the cease fire agreement with Government of India in Nagaland. But they have their designated camps at Ukhrul, Senapati and Chandel Districts of Manipur. The stand-off between Assam Rifles and the NSCN(IM) began on Sunday (18th January) night when soldiers of the country's oldest para-military force surrounded the banned outfit's camp at Kuisumong. They asked the rebels to vacate the area saying the cease-fire was only limited to Nagaland and no such camps were allowed in Manipur. The Naga Militants, however, refused to abide by the Assam Rifles' order and threatened to retaliate if the 'camp' was attacked.[26]

In such armed conflict situation of Siroy area, Tangkhul women came out and demanded scaling down of security forces and guerrillas. They make a vigil all the time during the tension and requested to both the parties and gave the massage of their motherly feelings and importance of the feeling of brotherhood to all the people. Lastly, the NSCN(IM) left the area and normalcy brought.[27]

All Tribal Women's Organisation, Chandel

There are 33 recognised tribes in Manipur. These different tribal communities are loosely grouped into two, i.e. Naga and Kuki (Chin Kuki Mizo). Some other minor tribes are also there who are claiming that they are not belonging to neither of the two. With the end of 1980s and with the beginning of 1990s, there was a communal clash between the Naga and Kuki. The worst effect of any communal clash or conflict is no one is looser or no one is gainer. But the problem suffered by both the communities. And again women of both the communities suffered all sorts of problems and difficulties directly or indirectly. They have lost their husband, brothers, sons, morality, all the properties and what not. In that situation, women were unable to remain in silence. They came out of the four walls of the houses and started to discuss about the problems. All Tribal Women's Organization, Chandel was formed during that time. There are around 12 tribes in Chandel district only. They have conducted different programmes like advocacy, peace building, training for understanding among male and female, interfered all the day to day happenings etc.[28] Simply they are trying to initiate all the conflicts and misunderstandings among the different communities in Manipur. Not only the communal conflicts or clashes, killing of innocent persons including women, rape including minor girl childs, bride burning etc. are increasing day by day in the social scenario of Manipur. Killing of five persons in different places of Manipur within a period of 20 days—February and March 2008 gave a serious blow to the minds of the people, specially the women activists in Manipur. All Tribal Women's Organization along with All Tribal Students' Women Organization and other civil society organizations launched a movement in March 2008 in connection with the killing of two tribal women of Chakpikarong in Chandel District. They have lodged the complain not only to the Government of Manipur and the Manipur State Women Commission, they wrote the incident in a clear way to the National Commission for Women demanding immediate punishment to the killers, compensation to the victims' family within an earliest date. It also called for a training of law enforcing agencies in human and gender rights. But unluckily they did not get any response upto the third week of April 2008. So, they have announced road blocked of National Highway No. 39, Imphal- Moreh road since Saturday 26-4-2008. On Monday 28-4-2008, they intensified their stir by closing down government offices in Chandel District.[29] As a response of the women's movement which was launched in an organized way, the Manipur Government, represented by Sri K. Ranjit Sing, Minister of Works negotiated with the agitators. By that time, Thoubal District Police arrested Amita (Majida) wife of Abdul Majid of Keirao Makha Leikai and Md. Tajuddin, son of (late) Allimuddin of Keibung Wangmataba in connection with the crime.[30] Consequently, they called of their strike, i.e. road blockade and closing of offices was finished.

Shree Digambar Jain Mahela Samaj

In Manipur not only the indigenous local women, those

women who are belonging to those communities who are coming from other states for earning their livelihood, i.e. for business purposes, also formed association or organizations here. Shree Digambar Jain Mahela Samaj is one among them. It was established in 1962 at Imphal. The main aims of the Samaj are to bring about social changes with the change of time and to give awareness of Jain religion to the new generation, particularly young boys and girls who were being educated in missionary schools. Even though this association or samaj is not a political body, they became active in different movements and agitations along with the other women organizations like Meira Paibies and other frontal organizations of the state like AMSU, Apunba Lup, AMUCO etc.

Some important activities of Shree Digambar Jain Mahela Samaj are as follows:

1. They joined AMSU and other organizations during the foreigner issue of 1980s.
2. They participated in the movement for inclusion of Manipuri language in the 8th Schedule of the Indian Constitution.
3. They joined the procession of 4th August, Integrity Rally of every year since 1997.
4. During the Anti-Cease Fire movement of June 2001, the Shree Digambar Jain Mahela Samaj was actively involved. They staged sit-in-protest at Jain Mandir Complex and used to seek slogans against the decisions of the government during night time along with the Meitei Meira Paibies. And they were so happy when the order of the government was changed.
5. They organized sit-in-protest for removal of Armed Forces Special Power Act, 1958.

6. They joined hands with other organizations in condemning merciless killing as well as give pressures to the government for finding out the real culprit and give a proper judgment of the cases like Netaji, Deepak Jain, Manoj Kumar Sethi, Sushil Sethi, L. Elizabeth, L. Bijoy Kumar.
7. They organized several '*Pujas*' (continuous for several days) and observed fasting for the peace and prosperity of Manipur.[31]

We find some typical social activities of women in Manipur, which are very identical and very purposeful and useful in the removal of social problems as well as welfare and development of the whole society. For each and every locality, mainly in the valley areas women are forming groups, which are popularly known as Nasha Bandi and Meira Paibi groups. They are strictly looking after the social problems of the local areas. When there is any hint for social evils like selling of drugs, alcohol, gambling, robbery, gender crimes etc. they voluntarily come out and joined together. They discussed about the matter and will decide what steps should be taken up. If necessary, they invite the local youth clubs and handover the case to the state police forces according to the cases.

As a result of the insurgency and counter-insurgency problems, people are totally confused in Manipur in certain cases. Youths are arrested and giving charges for involving with the underground organizations by giving proofs of pistols, hand grenades and other electronic equipments. The most puzzle things which are happening in the state, recently, are when the youths are arrested and not known whereabout of them, both the insurgents and counter insurgents are charging each other. The clear example of this case is the arrested and killing of K. Rishikanta Sing, a press reporter and resident of Kakwa, Imphal in November 2008. Before this there were a number of cases of above mentioned issues. People were arrested or kidnapped, then found nowhere or even found no clue for whereabout and sometimes found the death bodies.

During June-July 2008, there was a great tension in Manipur. Young boys and girls of below 15 years were arrested and one underground organization clarified that they joined their organization willingly. But the question of the society was how the children of below 15 years will work with the underground organization and if they are coming to join with the organization why that party does not make understand them. There was a great hue and cry about the issue. All the Meira Paibi groups, Nasha Bandi groups, clubs, organizations etc. came out and protested against the issue. They organized rally, sit-in-protest, seminar, open talks etc.

A protest rally was held on 17th March 2004, organized by the Chanura Lamchinglen Kangliepak, Human Rights Alert, COHAR, Threatened Indigenous People's Society, Meira Paibis. Their slogans were 'Indian Army Chatkhro', 'Mee Pharaga Hatkanu', 'Meecham Hatpa Shiphai Cheirak Piyu', 'Remove Armed Forces Special Power Act' etc. As the rally was joined by maximum public, it makes certain disturbance to the normal life of the Imphal Bazar. After the rally there was a public meeting which was jointly presided over by the President of Kanglamei, Y. Leirik; President of Meekhol, A.K. Janki; President of Poirei Leimarol Meira Paibi, L.Memchoubi.[32]

Another protest rally against the atrocities of the Assam Riffles on 2nd April at Keirak area as a result of the encounter between the undergrounds and the armed personnel was held at the evening of 3rd April 2004 in the rural areas. According to the protestant, encounter was between the underground and the Assam rifles, and the civil populace has no crime. So, Assam Rifles should not make any disturbance to the normal life of the public.[33]

So, in this way women in Manipur took active role in the

work of pressure groups in a democratic process. There activities are not only confined with the issues of women. They are not working in their own interest. They involved in all the issues which are related with the welfare and development of the society. They are taking care of the whole society. With the progress of human civilization, they got education, knowledge, ideas of progress etc. They become doctor, engineer, teacher, lawyer, scientist etc. but they are taking care of the society within the strict framework of their respective social norms. But until and unless they are mother, sister, sister-in-law etc. in their respective houses.

NOTES

1. *The Imphal Free Press*, Imphal, 27.4.1980.
2. *Economic and Political Weekly*, Mumbai, 24 July 2004, Editorial Caption "Odious comparisons", p. 3315.
3. *Times of India*, dated 5.3.2008, Anti-AFSPA stir gets support from Kerala.
4. Th. Binarani Devi, 'India's Look East Policy and Youths of Manipur', in Ray B. Dutta, Dev Bimal J., Sengupta Kiya, *Globalisation and North East India*, Concept Publishing Company, Pvt. Ltd. New. Delhi, 2008, pp. 320-21.
5. Pakem B., *Insurgency in North East India*, Omson Publications, New Delhi, 1997, p. V.
6. *Constitution*, All Manipur Nupi Marup.
7. *Times of India*, dated 19-2-2009, p.1, (Officers followed Chidambaram's Order till his last breath, *Times of India*, dated 10-1-2009, p.8.
8. *Poknapham*, Imphal, (Manipuri local daily), dated 23-2-2009, p1.
9. *Times of India*, 10-1-2009, p. 8 (Women Interrupted).
10. *Office record*, All Manipur Nupi Marup.
11. *Office record*, All Manipur Nupi Marup.
12. *Interviewed with Keinya Leima*, Founder President, Kha Nongpok Apunba Nupi Lup Moreh.
13. *Poknapham* (Manipuri Local Daily) dated 23-4-2009
14. *Office File*, All Manipur Social Reformation and Development Samaj, Imphal.

15. *Ibid*.
16. *Interviewed with Smt. K. Taruni Devi*, President, All Manipur Social Reformation and Development Samaj.
17. *Interviewed with Prof. Ksh. Bimola Devi*, President, Manipur University Working Women's Association, dated 6th February 2009.
18. *Interviewed with Dr. Kunjeshwori Devi*, Secretary, Manipur University Working Women's Association, dated 6th February 2009.
19. *Source, Office File*, Manipur University Working Women's Association.
20. *Interviewed with Bilorijan A.*, President, Ushoipokpi Tharaurok Women's Association, dated 10-2-2008.
21. *Interviewed with Kim Gangte*, dated.10-12-2008.
22. *Interviewed with Rose Mangshi Haokip*, President, Kuki Women's Union, dated 3-7-2008.
23. *Interviewed with Rose Mangshi Haokip*, President, Kuki Women's Union, dated 3-7-2008.
24. *Times of India*, dated 8-1-2008, p.4.
25. Zehol T.V.Lucy, 'Women's Movement in Manipur: Some Observations', in Karna M.N. (ed) *Social Movements in North-East India*, Indus Publishing Company, New Delhi, 1988, p.72.
26. *Times of India*, dated 23-1-2009.
27. *Interviewed with Ninghorla Zimik*, Ukhrul dated 2-2-2009.
28. *Interviewed with M. Shankilla, Secreatary*, All Tribal Women's Organisation , Chandel, dated 20-8-2008.
29. *Times of India*, dated. 29-4-2008, p. 4.
30. *Poknapham*, (Manipuri Local Daily), dated 30-4-2008, p. 1.
31. *Interviewed with Pramod Kumar Chhabra*, Member, Shree Digambar Jain Samaj, Imphal, dated 22-5-2008.
32. *Sangai Express*, Imphal Local Daily, English, dated 18-3-2004.
33. *Sangai Express*, Imphal Local Daily, English, dated 4-4-2004.

5

Impact of Women's Organization in a Democratic Society

India claims to be the worlds' biggest democracy and is respected by the whole world as the champion of non-violence and for having her political freedom achieved ultimately through non-violence. But this is especially true when it concerns the comfort, affluence, or power of any section and this profoundly affect all efforts of social reforms. The existence of the pluralistic type of society in modern times means the presence as well as the relevance of the innumerable variables and their proper representation. The formal structure of the government, executive, legislative and judiciary, as well as the party system have proved inadequate. On the other hand, a third approach of unofficial power has came into existence, i.e. the pressure groups.

The democratic liberalization, the latest, has not led to any real liberation of women in all societies of the world, particularly the Third World countries, largely due to the absence of supportive infrastructure that may facilitate women's empowerment. In a nutshell, the dominant patriarchal philosophy, the archaic traditions of the past, the obsolete middle class morals, false consciousness of liberation and the tight noose of modernism, fusionism and consumerism still obstruct the path of women's freedom. One important issue that challenges the existing romanticized understanding of empowered Manipuri women comes from the fact that women continue to be either silenced or deprived in terms of political representation. While historical legacies promise a fertile environment for women's participation in the modern representative form of politics, women's role is negligible other than exercising their periodic franchise. Present prevailing patriarchal social structure do not encourage women to be active in electoral politics. So far, not more than three women have been elected in the state legislative assembly of Manipur. On the other hand, ironically, one would witness women's active role at the grassroot, level as 'regular' activists as far as human security and human rights protection is concerned. Institution of 'Meira Paibi' and women's organization both registered and unregistered are illustrative example.

The democratic model did not develop theoretically in most of the Third World countries till only after gaining independence from colonial powers. The structure of political life for the ordinary women has largely remained hidden in the private sphere. Many feminists feel that democracy has failed to recognize women as political citizens in its theory and practice, and it has been more rewarding towards men than women. Third World women's liberation movements often have their origins in the national liberation movements. India is one of those countries where women achieved the status of political citizens without any opposition, as a part of political liberalism and sweeping reforms. In India, the year 1917 saw women agitating for the franchise under the leadership of Sorojini Naidu and demanded expansion in the education of girls. The number of girls' high schools was too low and they unequivocally condemned this discrimination. What the women wanted was equal status with men, and shared responsibilities. In 1926, women were given the right of membership of provincial legislature. Muthulakshmi Reddy was the first Indian women to be nominated Vice President of the Madras legislature and also first women doctor of graduate from Madras University. When the women entered into the socio-political process of the country, they started to take over the right, justice, equality etc. They set down some basic norms like, equal rights and obligation for all Indian citizens without sex bar; no disability to any citizen because of religion, caste, creed, or sex in regard to public appointment to an office of power, adult suffrage, women to contest an equal terms with men in mixed general election, etc.

Women's movements led to the democratization of society. In a democratization process, there should be an obligation for policy makers and security forces to be accountable to the public for their decisions and actions. Demobilizing the combatants and reintegrating them into normal life is one of the most challenging priorities in post conflict situations. In most cases, women are almost completely excluded from post conflict decision-making process. Women bring to peace process a practical understanding of real life and gender sensitivity. Today, peace process addresses the need for strengthening every democratic institutions where the real meaning of democracy can be achieved by all sections of people and protecting human rights.

Consequently, women have the right to vote and can contest the election. Even women members were there in the Constituent Assembly of India. In political sphere, India's women in general and Hindu women in particular, stood in the forefront of every movement. Modern Indian women are objects of admiration by people of the rest of the world for the role they have played in the country's public life. Women in India have not only reached the highest positions of power, and equal political and civil rights as men without having to fight for them, but they also have been increasingly joining the higher ranks of administration. When we start making a comparison between the role and status of women in modern

India and in the other countries of the world, particularly in the matter of emancipation of women, we are struck with unexpected contrasts. The part that has been played by Indian women in the freedom struggle and in the politics has been more important than that played by women in most other countries of the world. While their Western counterparts had to struggle to get political citizenship, Indian Women won the franchise at the same time as men, i.e. at the time of national independence in 1947, along with favourable legislation in many other areas. It was only in the late 1970s, that women realized that they were winners of a 'hollow fortress' as the social structures had largely remained unchanged. They have got the right to contest election just with the independence of India. Women were elected from the first Parliamentary election of 1952. But the number of women in governmental ministerial level is not increased with a desirable amount. And those countries where women received the political rights later than India are increasing the number of women in governmental ministerial level higher than India. Table 5.1 shows comparative figure of Indian women in political decision-making power along with some developing countries.

Table 5.1 : Women's Political Participation

Sl. No.	*Year women received rights*		*Year first women elected (E) or appointed (A) to parliament*	*Women in Governmental ministerial level*	*MDG Seats in Parliament held by women (% of total)*			*HDI rank*
					Lower or single house		*Upper house senate 2005*	
	To vote	*To stand for election*			*1990*	*2005*		
Botswana	1965	1965	1979E	26.7	5	11.1	-	131
Uganda	1962	1962	1962A	23.4	12	23.9	-	144
Namibia	1989	1989	1989E	19.0	7	25.0	26.9	125
Gabon	1956	1956	1961E	11.8	13	9.2	15.4	123
India	1950	1950	1952E	8.4	5	8.3	11.6	177

Source: Human Development Report, 2005.

The fifteenth Lok Sabha election is a fine blend of women in India. Although the women's researvation Bill proposing 33 per cent researvation for women in Parliament was not passed despite repeated attempts to table it, the new Lok Sabha has highest number of women MPs ever elected into the Lok Sabha. At 58, the 15th Lok Sabha has 13 more women MPs than the last House and nine more than the previous best of 49 in the 13th Lok Sabha. The representation of women members has crossed the 10 per cent mark for the first time in Indian history. However, this is still low in comparison with parliaments of the industrialized countries[1]. For instance,

UK	19.3%
USA	16.3%
Italy	16.1%
Ireland	14.2%
France	13.9%

For the first time in the electoral history of India in many years, we see the hope of youth, brimming with energy, guided by a clutch of experienced people of great maturity and sagacity. Some important young women Congress MPs, who have got success in this 15th Lok Sabha are—Mandasaur's Meenakshi Natarajan (36), Nagaur's Jyoti Mirdha (36), Bhiwani Mahendragarh's Shruti Choudhri (33) and Malda North's Mausam Noor (28) from different states and united by their agenda for development. The youngest MP of the 15th Lok Sabha is Agatha Sangma, 28 years, a woman MP from NCP of Meghalaya. Regarding the success of women MPs in the 15th Lok Sabha, intellectuals and eminent writers gave different comments. India's first woman IPS officer Kiran Bedi says things changed for the better when women enter a male dominated field. She said "After I joined the police force, it got more sensitized. Now, there are many women cops and more focus on women policing, even setting up of all-women *thanas*. Similarly, more women in Parliament will bring a different perspective to the House. Even in their respective constituencies, they will be sensitive about a different and a wider range of issues, and will tackle them with a new approach altogether." Author and political commentator Shobha De is cautious: "As an optimist, one would like to believe it's a positive change but it isn't always about the numbers. It is quality and commitment that count finally. I hope the new women parliamentarians focus on issues directly related to enhancing the lives of less privileged women in our country. A society is judged by the status of its women and unfortunately, our track record in this context has been dismal indeed."[2]

One important issue that challenges the existing romanticized understanding of empowered Manipuri women comes from the fact that women continue to be either silenced or deprived in terms of political representation. While historical legacies promise a fertile environment for women's participation in the modern representative form of politics, women's role is negligible other than exercising their periodic franchise. Present prevailing patriarchal social structure do not encourage women to be active in electoral politics. So far, not more than three women have been elected in the state legislative assembly of Manipur. Their participation in the electoral politics of Manipur is also just a shadow of their husbands. Here, I want to mean is Hangmila Sieza of Ukhrul Constituency captured the seat of her husband as a sympathy vote after the death of Sri Yangmaso Sieza, the former Chief Minister of Manipur. Smt. W. Leima Devi got the seat of her husband when he went to the Parliament. Smt. O. Landhoni Devi won the seat of her husband Sri O. Ibobi Sing left the seat when he became the Chief Minister. On the other hand, ironically, one would witness women's active role at the grassroots level as 'regular' activists as far as human security and human rights protection is concerned. Institution of 'Meira Paibi' and women's organization both registered and unregistered are illustrative example.

Women have to influence public opinion in favour of

their rights in sharing, inheriting and owning movable and immovable properties including land. Ultimately, the state could be pressurized to enact and implement suitable laws in honouring these rights of women. In fact women's organizations themselves should endeavour to create a space for themselves within the formal structure of political decision-making. Women from different angle launched not only the politicians and party members, different movements. All Manipur Nupi Marup joined in those movements. Since 1975, the All Manipur Nupi Marup observed International Women's Day with different programmes like conference, discussion, rally, demonstration etc. The main theme of the International Women's Day 1997 for the All Manipur Nupi Marup was the demand of Seat Reservation for Women in the Lok Sabha and State Legislative Assemblies. Inequalities in political power are directly or indirectly reflected by inequalities in income and human capabilities. Disadvantage groups—poor people, women, and rural populations, indigenous communities—are disadvantaged partly because they have a weak political voice because they are disadvantage where political institutions are seen as vehicles for perpetuating unjust inequalities or advancing the interests of elites, that undermines the development of democracy and creates conditions for state breakdowns.

The UN year of women and the decade that followed, made a qualitative change in the attitude of people towards women's problems. The International Decade for Women (1975-1985) heightened the awareness of people on the plight of Indian women. For the first time, unlike other resistance groups, a movement of women sprouted, who saw themselves as individuals in their own right. It was no more men crusading for women's issues but women and some sensitive men for women's issues. Lots of women's organizations emerged which aimed at conscientising everyone on women's issues and collectivizing experiences of the oppressed women to channelise the urge for change in the position of women in all spheres. The new consciousness gave rise to not only feminist (women and men) activists' but also feminist-activist-researcher. And a whole body of literature appeared and continued to pour day-in and day-out.[3] It led to a larger number of studies the world over on women's issues and brought out positive policy and legislative changes in respect to women's status, their rights and empowerment through state instruments. Even earlier, there have been women's organizations, both national and international, but afterwards their participation in women's struggle for securing gender justice increased substantially. Almost all nations established women's commissions and most universities recognized women's studies as important aspects of education and research. The woman was more visible, more vocal and more discussed in public debates and the media. The number of women candidates in the parliamentary and state legislative assembly elections are increasing even though the numbers of elected persons are not so increased. However, this did not mean that the fall out benefits of all this pervaded to the women of all sections, classes and continents. The women's movements in the Third World countries have always been limited to the middle class, and elite, largely urban based, restricted to the educated and economically well placed groups of women.[4]

Manipuri women are seen as tendrils in the breeze given to swaying rhythmically or as retiring housewives leisurely tucking at the looms. But they are much more. Perhaps, in the land of Chitrangada and Rani Gaidinliu, a woman militant; and Sharmila, a human rights activist; is nobody in particular. It is true that traditionally the Meitei women political status as such and the scope for their formally taking part in the decision-making process and in the affairs of the government as well as their rights in sharing the inheriting property did not commensurate with the vital role played by them in economic and cultural sphere. They are playing a vital role in the economic and cultural sphere of Manipur, but that situation has not resulted in the women acquiring absolute equality with men which they more than deserve. Manipur remains as much a man's world as it ever was.

When a political struggle in the land assumed popular character, it was inevitable that Manipuri women should ferment the dough with the yeast of their militancy. Yet the civil society protest movements organized by the women from time to time against unjust government decisions have impacted on the state policy in respect of human liberty. This may be reckoned as a significant feature of women power in Manipur. And the women of Manipur should actively deliberate on how they may be able to assert their rights in the political decision making system.

Since the passage of the 72nd and 73rd Amendments almost a million women have come into local politics. With the implementation of the 73rd Amendment Act, 1992, there is a scope for more democratic district administration in the shape of district government by vesting more powers and responsibilities in the self-governing bodies and involving the people in the making of their own destiny. These are indeed far reaching changes towards the realization of the dream of giving power to the people. But the State of Nagaland, Mizoram and Meghalaya remain out of the orbit of the 73rd Amendment and the hill areas of Manipur, where the district council minus the sixth scheduled provisions were once there, also do not come under the purview of the 73rd Amendment.[5] And, again, in Assam, Tripura and valley areas of Manipur, the issues raised by them at the grassroots level will have little success if women's representation in the upper echelons of democracy remains low. The question of 33 per cent reservation for women is still a hot issue in the Parliament of India. Women face immense challenges in participating in the political process. Prejudices and cultural perceptions deter women from contesting election. Those women who do enter politics have a tough time being taken seriously. Even they cannot get a life partner of their own when they became active politician, MLA or Minister. In Kolkata, a two time Marxist MLA, Mafusa Khatuns, from Kumarganj in South Dinajpur, was on the look out for a groom. If the match is good enough, Mafusa Khatun's family said, she may even quit politics and turn fulltime housewife. The last bit came as an after thought, when many prospective grooms reportedly backed out on learning her political inclination. The address, which came out recently in a Bengali Daily, did mention her as an MLA but skipped the CPM part. Offers have come from doctors, teachers and even an IPS officer. Assembly Speaker Hashin Abdul Halim understands her sentiments. It is not easy for conservative Muslim family to accept an MLA as a *Bahu*, he says, "otherwise politicians have glamour of their own and our male MLAs have no problems getting married. Since Mafusa had not been able to find a match of her own till now, her family members have a tough job at hand, particularly because she is a woman MLA".[6]

Still, women face immense challenges in participating in the political process. Prejudices and cultural perceptions deter women from contesting elections. Those women who do enter politics have a tough time being taken seriously. In India though the number of women MPs in the Lok Sabha is all time high of 49, this accounts for merely 9.1 per cent of all Lower House seats. No headway has been made on the controversial women's reservation bill to provide 33 per cent reservation for women in Parliament. It has helped build women's capacity and create new political leaders at local levels. This could translate into women emerging as leaders at the state and national level also. By getting more women into local councils, some of the structural barriers that prevent women from being elected may have been removed.

Progress towards democracy also has been mixed. Democracy is a fundamental aspect of human development.

It is both intrinsically valuable and, therefore, human development indicator in its own right, and a means towards wider human development goals. Measuring progress is inherently difficult. Multiparty elections—now the world's preferred form of governance—are one condition. An independent judiciary, constraints on executive power, freedom of the press and respect for human rights give substance to the form of electoral choice. By the Polity indicators of democracy, a composite benchmark, the share of the world's countries with multiparty electoral system that meet wider criteria for democracy has raised since 1990 from 39 per cent to 55 per cent.

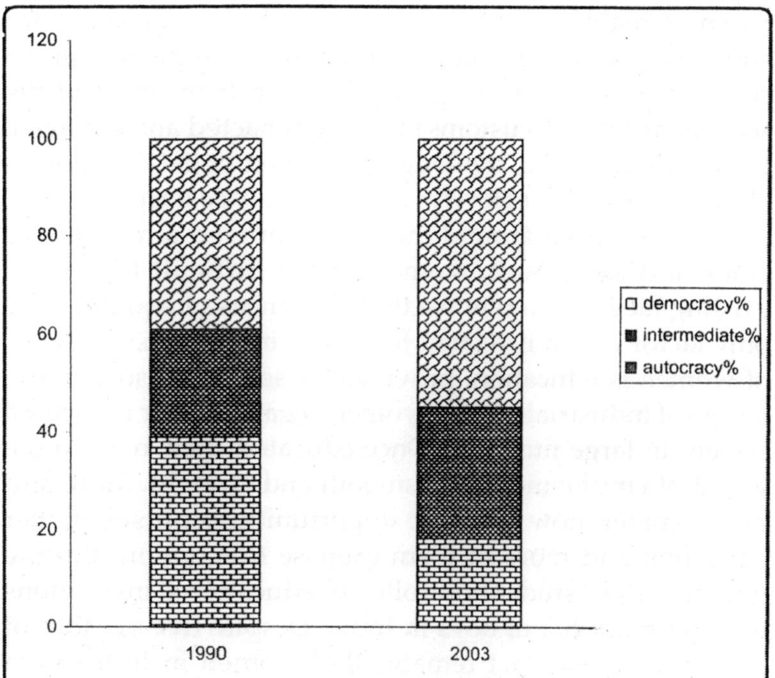

Source: Human Development Report, 2005.

Fig.5.1: Democracy gains ground

This represents an increase of 1.4 billion people living under multiparty democracy. But the pertinent question at this stage is how far multiparty politics is successed and can give the real meaning of democracy to the subjects. Is it really a democracy or monocracy? Many countries with multiparty elections are democracies in name and electoral autocracies in practice, with political leaders seen by their people as corrupt, tyrannical and predatory. Multiparty elections can provide a smokescreen that obscures over bearing executive power, limitations on press freedom and human rights abuses that strip democracy of its meaning. In some countries public protests has been a powerful antidote to such practices.

Constitutionally and legally, no barrier exists in women having equality with men, the principle for equal pay for equal work has been long accepted by all employers in the country; special laws to protect women from most of the socially degrading customs have been enacted and enforced. In spite of all these, the long established belief and notion about female inferiority and social prescription and prohibitions built around them have proved a hard nut to crack and as a result, women find it difficult to use the existing facilities to remove the hindrances of equality. The only factor which is related to change in the social position of women is education, provided by society to sustain the tempo of industrialization; women began to enter the school system in large numbers. Once educated their road to the world of employment was smooth and straight. More and more women now have the opportunity to pursue higher education and more of them exercise this option. But the number of girl students enrolled in educational institutions is lower than that of boys in India. Despite five decades of development the fact remains that women in India are a deprived section of society. Not only the benefits of development have eluded women as a category, in some ways development processes have enhanced male domination over women and added to their deprivation.

Opportunities for education have increased but the rate of female literacy and enrolment in educational institutions is much less than men. Table 5.2 shows the gender difference or inequality in education.

Table 5.2: Gender Inequality in Education

Adult literacy		Youth literacy		Net Primary enrolment		Net secondary enrolment		Gross tertiary enrolment	
Female rate% age 15 and above) 2003	*Female rate as % of male rate 2003*	*Female rate (% ages 15-24) 2003*	*Female rate as % of male rate 2003*	*Female ratio (%) 2002-03*	*Ratio of female to male 2002-03*	*Female ratio (%) 2002-03*	*Ratio of female to male 2002-03*	*Female ratio (%) 2002-03*	*Ratio of female to male 2002-03*
47.8	65	67.7	80	85	0.94	–	–	10	0.68

Source: Human Development Report, 2005.

The cultural image of women, the position occupied by her at a particular time is determined to a great extent by her education. The desire for a higher standard of living and consequent acceptance of women's employment has also been a factor in creating a positive attitude towards women's education.

Education is not simply about jobs. Education is also about access to new knowledge, information and ideas as well as the capacity to use these effectively. These are enhacements of the capabilities that indiduals bring to their goals in many areas of life, aside from the labour market. They explain some aspects of the correlation between women's education and various human development outcomes referred to earlier.

Women may have an impact on power relations within the home. In Sierra Leone and Zimbabwe, educated women were found to have more leverage in bargaining within their families and husbands and a greater say in spending household income than uneducated women. In rural

Bangladesh, educated women in rural areas were likely to participate in a wider range of decision-making than uneducated women.

Educated women also appear less likely to suffer from domestic violence. A study from Calcutta in West Bengal notes that educated women were better able to deal with violent husbands. Access to secondary stages of education may have an important contributory role in enhancing women's capacity to exercise control in their lives through a combination of literacy and numeracy skills, and enhanced self-esteem.[7]

A similar finding was documented in rural Bangladesh. Women put a great deal of emphasis on education for their daughters. This is to ensure that the daughters will be able to stand up to their husbands and have the resources to fall back on should they ever need to become independent. The value given to education and how it is utilized will be mediated within the wider context in which it is provided. These are other less positive findings from some studies.

Indeed, findings from rural India, a mother's education may also result in unequal reduction in the mortality risk of boys and girls, further widening the differentials. The power relations embodied in the delivery of education must also be considered. This is particularly the case in the formal educational system and represents a second set of qualifications concerning education as a route to women's empowerment. The content of education often serves to mirror and legitimize wider social inequalities.

Formal educational content often denigrates physical labour, largely the preserve of the poor; and domestic activities, largely the preserve of women. Gender stereotyping in the curriculum, particularly in text books, serve to reinforce traditional gender roles within society and to act as a barrier to the kind of futures that girls are able to imagine for themselves. Indeed, the design of education has often reinforced the biases of many parents that the purpose of schooling is to prepare girls for their domestic roles.

Of late, the most effective channels for change appear to be those that are set up by women themselves, drawing on their collective memories of shared lives. In Manipur, like most of the countries around the world, females through their collective action and memberships in solidarity groups and grassroots organizations have been able to challenge the age old conventions having a bearing on their lives. While it is the traditional support system together with organized effort that seems to have helped the rural females the most, in the urban context, access to education, skill formation and paid employment lending a sense of empowerment equip women to enter into a bargaining position with prevailing norms of patriarchy.

The social status of women are reflected in the custom relating to marriage, religion and property, widowhood, dowry, role in the family, basic attitudes with respect to the social image of women etc. Even though this position continued in the beginning of the British period, the spread of English Education which was a characteristic of British Rule and the intermixture of Western and Eastern cultures enabled women to realize their subordinate position and persuaded them to regain their legitimate status. The various Hindu Revivalist organizations, such as the Arya Samaj and the Brahmo Samaj gave a great impetus to the awakening of womanhood. Educated women came forward demanding equal rights with men, Rambai Ranade, Pandita Ramabai, Sarala Devi, Chonda Rani, Shreemathi Saroj Nalini and host of others are known for their valuable service for uplifting the position of women during this period. With the progress of human civilization, women today are breaking the social psychological barriers and are assuming new responsibilities. Women's economic horizon once confined to domestic servanthood or labour on the farm has expanded considerably. Women from all shades of life started working in other fields. They are now employed as teachers, doctors, lawyers, nurses, engineers, journalists, officers in the government departments and commercial houses. The growing participation of women in the economic development of the country is reflected from the fact that in the organized sector the number of women employees has increased considerably at the national level. The growing economic participation of women in the economic development of India is reflected from the fact that in the organized sector the number of women employees has increased considerably from 13.7 lakh in 1962 to 24.4 lakh in 1975 then 28.57 lakh in 2000.

There appears to be a perceptible shift in women's agency as result of entry into waged labour opportunities generated by the expansion of non-traditional agricultural exports. However, changes in women's life chances as a result of entry into waged work appear more marked when the focus is on the non-agricultural sector. This is partly because such employment is generally associated with migration by women out of rural areas and away from the patriarchal control of kinship and community.

The division of labour in domestic chores and childcare is rarely renegotiated across the genders. Despite their increased labour input into paid work, women (particularly married women) either continued to bear the main burden of domestic work, or share it with other female members of the household, often their daughters. By and large, gender inequalities in work burdens appear to be intensified. The attention to export oriented manufacturing and agriculture should not detract attention from an important fact of life. The vast majorities of working women do not work in these sectors but are to be found in the informal economy concentrated in the most casualised forms of waged labour and low value own account enterprises. There has been a great deal of controversy about whether labour standards including the right to organize, can be improved through trade sanctions. Whatever the outcome of this debate, however, the reality remains. Globally enforced labour standards will do little to change the lives and livelihoods of the vast majority of working women in the informal economy where such standards are impossible or impossibly expensive, to enforce. A more inclusive approach would be to institute a universal social floor based on supporting all and supporting by all.

In both public and private organized sectors at all India level, there has been a marginal increase in 2001 from 2000. In terms of percentage changes, Manipur recorded a positive change of 1.5 per cent in 2000 and 2001 while national figure was 0.5 per cent only. Increase of women workforce in the organized sectors indicates that women are becoming more aware and educated. Organized sector, here, is understood as those parts of the economy which operate through institutions which feed figures into official statistics, details of which are accessible. One typical situation of Manipur is it is economically backward state and private investors shy away; being so, existence of companies with potentials job creation is low. Thus, opportunity of working in the organized private sector is less in the state. The dominant framework of women's contribution largely ends up making a passing reference to women and their role. This dominant perspective has also successfully created a romanticized image of Manipuri women which in turn has weakened the possibility of rethinking on the existence of poverty, displacement, trauma and low social status, which are historically embedded in the social structures. One cannot outrightly deny the role of women in the economy of Manipur.

Globalization affects mainly the women in the unorganized sectors, if their products are pushed to the export markets or if the high technology replaced their hand crafted products to assembly line items. The most basic capabilities for human development are leading a long and healthy life, being educated and having adequate resources for a decent standard of living. Other capabilities include social and political participation in society. The era of globalization has been marked by dramatic advances in technology, trade and investments—and an impressive increase in prosperity. Gains in human development have been less important. Large parts of the developing world are being left behind. Human development gaps between rich and poor countries, already large, are widening. Meanwhile, some of the countries most widely cited as examples of globalization 'success stories' are finding it harder to convert rising prosperity into human development. Progress in reducing child mortality, one of the most basic of human development indicators, is slowing and the child death gap between rich and poor countries is widening. For all of the highly visible achievements, the reach of globalization and scientific advance falls for short of ending the unnecessary suffering, debilitating diseases and death from preventable illness that blight the lives of the world's poor people. On average, people born in a developing country today can anticipate being wealthier, healthier and better educated than their parents' generation. They are also more likely to live in a multiparty democracy and less likely to be affected by conflict. In a little more than a decade average life expectancy in developing countries has increased by two years. On this indicator human development is converging: poor countries are catching with rich ones.

Women's participation in paid work is a strong correlate of poverty in both urban and rural areas in many parts of the world. This is most evident in those places where powerful social norms restrict women's ability to take employment in the public sphere. In countries such as Bangladesh, India and Pakistan, female labour force participation is highest in the poorest households and tends to decline as households become better off. It is not that women stop working, but that their work takes a different form and happens in a different place from the public spheres-home-based and often unpaid.

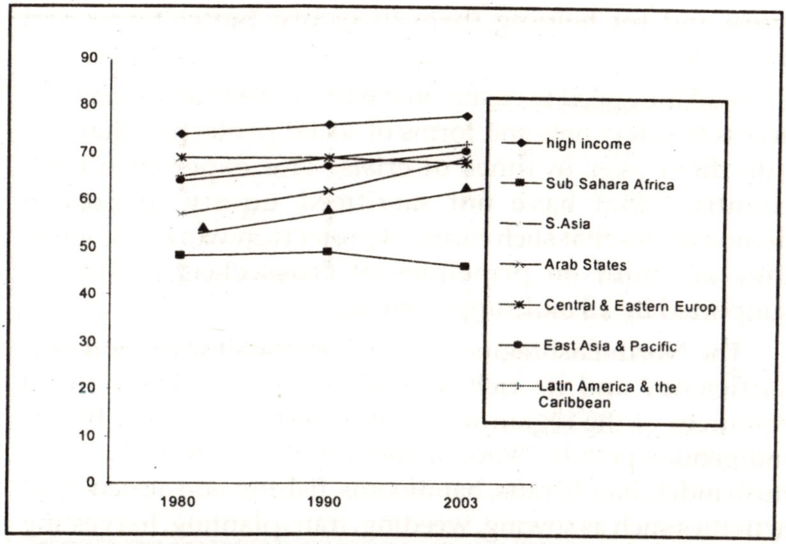

Source: Human Development Report, 2005.

Fig. 5.2: Life expectancy improving in most regions of the world

Elsewhere, domestic responsibilities may constrain women's ability to access labour market opportunities, but not prevent them from taking up paid employment in the public domain. The relationship between women's employment and household poverty is likely to be somewhat different in these contexts.

Women are now active in wage labour on a historically unprecedented scale but at a time when labour markets have become increasingly deregulated and labour increasingly reduced to the status of a commodity. The goals of both poverty eradication and gender equality demand, not those women are privileged over men in access to employment, but that both are able to access decent forms of work and on the same terms. Policy makers need to consider both the quantity of employment available to the poor and to poor women in particular, as well as the quality. They need to consider measures for improving the returns to women's work and for helping them to secure better terms and conditions.

And they need to ensure that both women and men have access to safety nets and forms of social protection that will tide them over in times of crisis. The experience from countries that have not sacrificed equity to growth demonstrates that such forms of protection work best when they are built on principles of cross-class solidarity, supported by all and supporting all.

The North East region was well known for its food self-sufficiency and its rich natural resources. The natural resources of the region were harnessed sustainably by the indigenous people. Wood gathering, livestock and animal husbandry, handicrafts, handlooms, fishing and agricultural activities such as sowing, weeding, transplanting, harvesting and post-harvesting activities like thrashing, husking, grinding etc. were undertaken by our rural women. After the liberalization of economy and in the new circumstances created by SAP for globalization, the traditional role of women is being undermined whereas mechanization and automation is becoming prevalent in the market based economy which has adversely affected the village based traditional economy. The opening of markets led to the commercialization of agriculture and new technologies penetrated into our agricultural lands. But in this context too regarding upgradation of agricultural development tools women were neglected. The transmission of knowledge about the new technologies like use of tractors, high quality fertilizers, selection of HYV seeds, pesticides etc. became man-to-man affairs. Men were increasingly drawn into the modernizing agriculture sector while women stayed in subsistence agriculture with no access to credits, training and technologies. The agricultural development has normally and almost entirely been manned by men right from the decision making to implementation.[8] Again women have also been excluded from owning or controlling land, even after the implementation of the Right to Property Act, 2005, the most crucial productive resource in agricultural economies. Earlier women and men were equal partners in agriculture. Their knowledge and contribution and participation in decision-making were recognized. But with the commercialization of agriculture, women's job is taken up by men and mechanization has displaced a large segment of agricultural work.

When such women lose the employment opportunities they suffer both as producers, with suddenly no earnings, or as consumers with no purchasing power because of escalating prices of imported mass produced products of home consumption. Manipuri women's encounter with modern political economy, similar to other women's across the globe, reflect some of the contradictions inherent in finance capitalism under the prevailing system of neo-liberal economic policy and ensuing structural violence. As a result of the structural adjustment programme initiated since the early 1990s in India, women have started to face displacement and deprivation. Displacement can be visibly observed over the North East India as the forces of globalization, privatization and liberalization acting through Public and Private Corporations, backed by the Indian state's overt nation building exercise and its encroaching hegemony over local economy is ousting indigenous women's markets and production centres. Poverty is being created, intensified and deliberately entrenched. In its new avatar, States seeks to perpetrate feminized poverty. Bulldozing of Sana Keithel or Khwairamband Bazar in recent times to construct a multi-storied market building is a case in point that explicates how neo-liberal forces have cordoned off the hitherto accessible place to all classes of women (petty traders).[9] Worklessness, malnutrition, drudgery and marginalization mark the women's lot in the Third World societies. During October November 2008, with an order of the Government of Manipur, the women vendors of Khwairamband Bazar were vacated. That disturbed a lot to the petty traders. So, they called bands and hartals in the Bazar area.

The recent process of globalization is more pervasive, penetrating and plightful. The wide opening up of the markets and hegemonisation of the multinational corporations lead to ruthless de-humanization of plural cultures by modern technology and multimedia communications. Understanding women's role in the economy and sustainable equity based development calls for an approach that would critique the existing oppressive forms of labour. The non-recognition of women's domestic labour as productive denies the possibility for rightful share of resources and dignity in the society. The labour force contributed by women is higher than that of men. In the work sector women's labour at home is not recognized at all.

The Indian Constitution and protective laws assert equity and justice to be the goals but the given socio-economic and political system and shared understanding between men and women in preordained situations assign different kinds of resources, opportunities and expectations to the two sexes, each of which is sought to be governed by its own distinct code of fairness and justice. As every working women knows, enjoying equal rights to employment does not lesser her burden of domestic duties. The concept of equality and justice results in gross injustice to women. An ILO study estimated that unpaid household work was 25.39 per cent of the total gross national product in developing countries. There has been minimal involvement of local and national programmes. Therefore, there was an urgent need to develop gender-wise data whenever necessary, for effective decision-making. Women occupy a very law position in organized employment sectors as compare to men. Even there, they are subjected to other forms of discrimination such as comparatively low wages, longer working hours, restricted career prospects etc. They performed many activities at home and outside whose economic value goes unnoticed and unrecognized. It is invisible labour at the most. Table 5.3 clearly shows the gender, work and time allocation in India.

Table 5.3: Gender, work, and time allocation in India, 2000

Total work time Min. per day		*Female work time (% of male)*	*Time allocation*					
			Total work time		*Time spent by women*		*Time spent by men*	
Women	*Men*		*Market activity*	*Non-market activity*	*Market activity*	*Non-market activity*	*Market activity*	*Non-market activity*
457	391	117	61	39	35	65	92	8

Source : Human Development Report, 2005.

Understanding the causes and consequences of gender inequality, therefore, and the power relations that generates and is generated in the process, should be of concern to all socities in the world, rich as well as poor. The pervasiveness of gender inequality cuts across all other forms of socio-economic differentiation. It is a feature of rich as well as poor groups, racially subordinate groups, privileged as well as untouchable castes. The intersection of gender discrimination with economic deprivation tends to produce intensified forms of disadvantage, more often for women and girls than for men and boys.

Now-a-days women have taken up various professions both in the government and in the private sectors and are doing very well. To mention some of the careers where women from this region are performing very well in nursing, teaching, banking, bureaucracy, medical, engineering, law, police, defence, music, media, politics, journalism etc. Those women who have skills and access to credit are taking up several self-employment activities as their career like Tailoring, Petty Shops, and other micro-enterprises like Grinding, Processing, Beauty Parlours etc. The emerging institutions that impart vocational training such as fashion technology and design, fabric painting, interior decoration and beautician courses have attracted the women folk of this region who undergo training and establish their own enterprises. This has led to the growth of employment and women's career.[10]

Women in North East India are so conscious of the socio-economic conditions and think how to earn money and manage the household chores. But they are at the same time face multiple problems. This does not change her role expectations of the parents-in-law. They still have the expectations from their daughter's-in-law in various matters. In some cases husbands also expect the same kind of attention from her although she is in gainful employment. If she carries out single handedly all the traditional duties and responsibilities at home and does the duties at work place, she becomes over strained and tired. She suffers also from mental and physical depression and fails to provide pleasant and enjoyable companionship to her husband and children. Vast majority of educated women still perceived their lives in terms of having children and looking after the homes. To them, professional work is secondary and family is of primary significance. This leaves their educational attainment to disuse.[11]

They are workers in both spheres—those most responsible and therefore with most at stake, those who suffer most when the two spheres meet at cross-purposes, and those most sensitive to the need for better integration between the two. It is this positioning of women at the intersection of productive and reproductive activities that gives rise to potential synergies and trade-offs which policy makers need to be aware of in their attempts to achieve the MDGs (Millennium Goal Development). It also means that the MDGs, each of which relate to a particular form of deprivation or shortfall, cannot be achieved in isolation from the structural inequalities which gave rise to them. If gender inequality is part and parcel of the processes of poverty and discrimination in a society, it must figure just as integrally in the set of measures to eradicate this condition.[12]

It is ironical that much has been written about women's contribution but such writings have largely failed to actually deepen the understanding on the needs and deprivation of women. The truth is that dominant framework largely ends up making a passing reference to women and their role. Public policies should be gender sensitive. For example, technology can be introduced in such a way in which opportunity exists where women can adapt and learn.[13] As the wearer knows where the shoe pinches clearly the problems of women can easily acknowledge by the womenfolk. The contributions made by women should be acknowledged by the whole society.

Women's movement, therefore, have to save women from further marginalization and provide empowerment for achieving self-respect, equity and equality.[14] An important factor attracting more and more women to employment is the hard economic necessity. In the urban middle and lower middle classes this is very much the case. Some women from the middle and upper middle classes take up employment to improve the standard of living of the family through augmenting the family income. This has already begun to exert an influence on the middle class women. Under the pressure of economic necessity, opposition to the gainful occupation of women is steadily diminishing even among traditionally minded orthodox and conservative groups.

A woman has great capacity to work but, she suffers a lack of self-confidence, which includes the society she lives in, to create the right kind of situation. There are four important needs :

1. Need to create awareness in the society of the social ills.
2. The law enforcement agencies should be made more effective and trained to tackle the problem in the right perspective.

3. Necessary changes should be made in the procedure and machinery of administration so as to get the desired results.
4. Need to provide socio-economic security of women.

As a response to the above requirements, different departments and agencies of the government started to take up programmes and works for the development of women and the society as a whole. As for instance, the Labour Bureau brings out a publication entitled *Women in Employment* presenting a picture of the trends of women's employment in India. The Ministry of Programme Implementation was created in September 1985 for effective monitoring of the implementation of certain projects and programmes. A Department of Personnel and Training was set up which collects and publishes data on women employees' representation in various services in government. Some of the major initiatives taken up by the Government of India towards removing various gender biases to ensure that women enjoy equal status *vis-à-vis* men in the real sense as enshrined in the Constitution of India are as follows :

(1) Enactments Passed:

I. Child Marriage Act, 1976.
II. Equal Remuneration Act, 1976.
III. Dowry Prohibition Act, 1961.
IV. Immoral Traffic (Prevention) Act, 1986.
V. Indecent Representation of Women (Prohibition) Act, 1986.
VI. Commission of Sati (Prevention) Act, 1987.
VII. Medical Termination of Pregnancy Act, 1971.
VIII. Pre-natal Diagnostic Techniques (Regulation and Prevention of Misuse) Act, 1992.

IX. 72nd and 73rd Amendments to the Constitution—Reservation of seats for women in Panchayats and Municipalities.
X. Women's Right to Property Act, 2005.
XI. Domestic Violence Act, 2005.

(2) The Government of India sets up exclusive Department of Women and Child Development in 1985 and the following organizations:

I. National Institute of Public Cooperation and Child Development;
II. Central Social Welfare Board;
III. Rashtriya Mahila Kosh;
IV. National and State Commissions for Women;
V. The Standing Committee on 'Empowerment of Women' set up by Parliament.

(3) In connection with the gender issues, programmes are initiated by different Departments and Agencies of the Government.

I. ***The Department of Women and Child Development***: The notable programmes are—Indira Mahila Yojana (IMY); Hostels for Working Women; Short-stay Home for Women and Girls; Mahila Samridhi Yojana (MSY); Gender Sensitization and Awareness Generation; Support of Training and Employment Programme for Women (STEP); Training-*cum*-Employment-*cum*-Production Centres; Balika Samridhi Yojana; etc.
II. ***Central Social Welfare Board***—Condensed courses of Education and Vocational Training; Socio-economic Programme for Women; Crèches for Working/Ailing Mothers' Children; Family Counselling Centres.
III. ***National Commission for Women***: A statutory body was set up under a Central Act in 1992, the

Commission strives to achieve equity, equality and justice; pursues gender justice through intervention in case of violation of equality, denial of opportunities and deprivation of women's right. It arranges counselling and assistance to women victims of atrocities and women in distress all over the country.

IV. ***The Manipur State Commission for Women*** : It was set up as a statutory body on September 15, 2006 at the state level in pursuance of the Manipur State Commission for Women Act, 2006. Its mandate is very wide by covering all aspects of women's development. The Commission visited remote hilly and village areas of Manipur and conducted counselling and advocacy programmes with the women of those respective areas. It also highlighted the issues and challenges of women in different sections of different communities. It receives cases and complains of crimes against women. The Chairperson and Members of the Commission called upon both the parties and negotiated; then tried to a compromised and understanding between them if possible. It takes the helps of different departments of the state government like police, legal courts, medical etc.

(4) The Government of India took up some policies and programmes advocating women's concerns—National Plan of Action for Women 1976; National Perspective Plan for Women (1988-2000); Shram-Shakti Report of the National Commission on Self-Employed Women and Women in the Informal Sectors; National Policy for the Empowerment of Women (Draft) Plan of Action to combat Trafficking and Commercial Sexual Exploitation of Women and Children.

As a response to the above mentioned initiatives of the

government, as well as with the cooperation and responsibilities of women , we can see some impacts of the plans, policies; and programmes increasing the status of women.

Table 5.4 : Status of women

	In 1951	*In 1991*
Expectancy of Life for Females	31.6Yrs	61.5 (1996)
Mean Age of Marriage for Girls	15.6Yrs	18.3 Yrs
Infant Mortality Rate	131	75 (1993)
Literacy Rate for Females	8.86%	39.19%
Enrollment of Girls in Schools	5.4mn	46.4mn (1993-94)
Women's Participation Rate	14.22%	22.27%
Women in Organised Sector	19.3 lakhs (in 1971)	40.27lakhs (in 1993)

The government in collaboration with different governmental agencies and NGOs made some future programmes in connection with the raising of the status of women, gender equality and social justice—Adopting National Policy for the Empowerment of Women; Convergence of Women Development Programme at the Central and State level; Setting up Office of the Commissioner for Women's Rights; Setting up National Resource Centre for Women.

Women's movements have a great contribution in the socio-economic and political development of the society. In some societies like Manipur, women's movements are not originated with the issues of women concerned. They have dealt with the whole socio-political and economic conditions of the society. With the progress of civilization as well as experiences they also acknowledged about the position and the role of women. They also became aware of the fact that if the conditions of the women are not improved then the welfare and development of the society will have no meaning. As they are contributing nearly halve of the total populations, their role is so important in a democratic society. The women of Manipur are now politically conscious and often resort to various forms of agitations in a democratic way and trying to get the real meaning and fruits of democracy. In every demonstration, female participation constitutes about 50 per cent and above of the total population. There are some movements that are launched by women only. In the mass movements too they think that their participation is compulsory. We can also observe at present that though women came out actively on many issues, they hardly succeed and attain their goal on some of the important social issues. One important factor responsible for their failure is the appeasing policy of the ruling party. Many political leaders often employed and misguided them for their interests and advantages. This created many factions and led to groupisms. The other factor is the prevailing law and order situations in Manipur which hampers the execution of their work.[15]

If women suffer various forms of inequalities and discrimination at home, then their plight outside the home is equally worst. Violence against women is committed at workplaces, educational institutions, in public transport, and on streets. Such crimes against women have become so pervasive that recently the Supreme Court gave a comprehensive definition of crimes against women was set up which collects and publishes data on women employees' representation in various services in government.

Indian women now understand most issues even if they hail from the lowest economic strata. They have the fact and personage which gets reflected in the women related studies of sociologists, economists and pursuers of allied scientific endeavours, irrespective of the fact whether the database of these studies have been collected by NGOs, Universities and Researchers, or by the census and other agencies connected with women and child welfare in diverse sectors. The political awakening of the freedom movement provided the renaissance of the Indian womanhood.

Pressure groups are both 'natural and necessary'. It is natural for people with similar or identical interests to combine and put up a united front. Without organization, their common problems would not get adequate representation. When they are united, it became a great force and got the ideas and they exchanged each other. The pressure groups retain a firm grip on their members and thus impose the much needed discipline. Pressure groups do not operate in a vacuum. Against every pressure group, there is a countervailing power. For instance, both the employers and the employees have pressure groups which keep the balance nearly even. Moreover, civil service, cabinet and the Prime Minister naturally put a brake to all unreasonable demands or pressure in Britain. Pressure groups help policy formulation; they are the barometer of various interests in the community. They represent the enlightened self-interest and also help the government in the implementation of certain important national policies. Even though pressure groups are not the parties which are not contesting in the election, but the target structure of pressure group involve the entire paraphernalia of a modern legislative organization beginning from electoral struggles to the point of policy formulation. Their role may be discovered in the writings of political manifestoes, distribution of election tickets and the formulation of legislative policy.

After having a clear analysis of the activities of women organizations as a pressure group, we can proudly say that their activities are part and parcel of the activities of government in a democratic process. There are three main points of significance of the study of pressure groups in the political process of a democratic society.

1. They are of numerous advantages to political parties and thereby contribute to the sustenance of the modern representative system. Power corrupts man and power alone checks power. The pressure groups thus act as a powerful check upon the arbitrary exercise of power and as they themselves are prone

to abuse their share of power, it is essential that various pressure groups be allowed to act as a check upon one another in order to establish and sustain the system of 'check and balances'. It also implies that when the groups act as a check upon the government, the latter must see to it that the activity of group politics is saved from deterioration to the extent of vitiating or destroying the political system itself.

2. The utility of pressure groups must be examined in the light of new approach to the meaning of politics. Politics is a struggle for power creating conflicts and offering their solutions and adjustments.
3. It will give a chance for a participatory democracy not a representative democracy. With the help of the process of pressure groups all sections of people can take part in the democratic process even though they are not entering into the formal process of the decision making process.

NOTES

1. *Times of India*, dated,19-5-2009. p.6
2. *Times of India*, dated, 26-5-2009, p.5.
3. Andal, N. *Women and Indian Society—Option and Constraints*, Rawat Publication, Jaipur, p.176.
4. *Ibid.*, p.184
5. Th. Binarani Devi, 'Position, Power and Functions of Women in Kuki Society', in Ray B. Dutta and Ray Asok Kumar (ed.) *Dynamics of Power Relations in Tribal Societies of North-East India*, Om Publications, New Delhi, 2006, p.199.
6. *Times of India*, dated 28-10-2007, p.1, "Wanted: Suitable boy for MLA".
7. Sarkar, Aanchal, *Gender and Development*, Pragun Publications, New Delhi, 2006, p, 46.
8. Phukon, Dolly, 'New Economic Policy and Its Impact on Traditional Skills of Women in North East India', ir Day B. Dutta, Dev Bimal J.(ed) *Globalization and North East India*, Concept Publishing Company Pvt.Ltd., New Delhi, 2008 p. 349.

9. Haripriya Soibam, 'Invisible Workforce: Women in the Economy of Manipur', in *Alternative Perspectives, Economy, Polity, History and Culture,* Vol. III, Issue.
10. Sengupta, Surojit, Career of Women in North East India: An Overview, in Ray Basudeb Dutta and Ray Asok Kumar (ed), *Women Emancipation, Focus North East India,* Om Publications, New Delhi, 2008, p.106.
11. *Ibid.,* p. 107.
12. Sarkar, Aanchal, *Gender and Development,* Pragun Publications, New Delhi, 2006, pp. 34-35.
13. Haripriya, Soibam, *op. cit.,* p. 43.
14. Andal, N. *op cit,.* p. 182.
15. Zehol. Lucy, 'Women's Movement in Manipur: Some Observation', in Karna, M. N. (ed.). *Social Movements in North-East India,* Indus Publishing Company, New Delhi, 1988, p. 73.

6

Conclusion

Women organization at the forefront of civil society movements in India have had notable successes in areas like social and political changes, economic reforms, human rights protections etc. It is the function of the women organization in collaboration with other civil society organizations to observe and critically evaluate and put checks on the activities of the government towards the subjects. With the increasing power and influence of the civil society organizations and sometimes as a result of their acts of extremism, they were not given access to government information and statistics and were branded as anti-national and unlawful organizations. In the 1990s, as international pressure mounted, the government was forced to give access to international organizations like Amnesty International to investigate instances of human rights abuses.

Agencies have to be exercised on a collective basis if such changes are to translate into structural transformation. It is necessary, therefore to look towards new forms of association which can bring women into the public domain to collectively challenge patriarchal power across a wide range of institutional spheres. There is, of course, nothing inherent to associations which make them vehicles for the promotion of gender equality goals, whether they are women's organizations or not.[1]

Many may be specifically set up to protect an elitist *status quo* or to promote a welfarist agenda for women. Equally, however, others can help to expand the space available for democratic activity. These groups may not necessarily operate in the political sphere, but they become 'democratically relevant' when they seek to contest relations of dominance within their own sphere of operation.

Struggle to improve the public provision of social services, to render them more responsive to the needs of the poor, may also be counted as a part of the process of building and strengthening citizenship identity. Thus, it is not simply the formally constituted political organizations which are relevant to the practice of citizenship. All forms of organizations and pressure groups that succeed in building the conditions which would enable citizens to act as citizens are relevant and necessary.

Examples of collective action and social mobilization that have succeeded in giving voice to women as well as men, from poorer sections of the population, can be found in many contexts and take many forms. These includes:

1. To organize awareness, sensitization and mobilization programmes for women.
2. Self-help groups and micro credit groups formed around microfinancial services of various kinds.
3. Labour organizations that have sprung up to address the interests of women working in different sectors, including the informal economy.
4. Social movements around issues such as fair access to land, water and other vital resources.
5. Initiatives to promote greater awareness about HIV/AIDS, which becomes a campaign for sex workers' rights.

Extensive training programme should be undertaken in

order to upgrade the traditional skills of women in artistic works so that their products can compete in the open markets. Special programme should be undertaken for health and nutritional improvement of women. Women in NE states, particularly the tribal women, are ahead in some respects. It requires nurturing of their inherent strength and leadership qualities reflected during the freedom struggle and their struggle against violation of human rights. Tribal women have disproved the artificial demarcation between man and woman and have proved that domestic and public spaces are equal for them. Movements of the sub-nationalities have enlightened the society and have brought many women in the public sphere cutting across the sex based rigidities and fundamentalism. The knowledge revolution need be extended further in the society for the emancipation of women.[2]

Liberty and freedom of women are suppressed by the tyranny of society often represented by social groups of tribal chiefs. In the tribal society of north-eastern states the wind of modernism is blowing over all the communities. Their culture and modes of life are in the process of transition. The north-eastern societies have an inherent social power of women that is often suppressed by ethnic clash, illiteracy, lack of employment and earning avenues. Now in the transitional phase they are handicapped in different ways. They in most of the cases do not have property rights, employment opportunities outside agriculture and in many cases, not even a settled household life.[3]

Today, the state and civil society organizations are engaged in a somewhat complex choreography with one another, sometimes in co-operation—as when the government contracts social services or data collection to them—and sometimes at conflict with each other. In certain cases, to provide political cover for it regard in the infringement of rights, the government tends to dismiss NGO reports as lacking objectivity and credibility, and often projects NGOs through strict applications of the Foreign Contributions Regulations Acts (FCRA) and curtailing the flow of foreign funds and assistance for NGOs.[4]

Civil society include the modern incarnations of traditional social institutions of the tribal communities, churches, human rights groups, bar associations and intellectuals, women's, students and youth groups. Women's groups find an important seat at the table, reflecting the growing understanding of the need to specifically pay attention to gender perspectives on conflict and peace, and to enable women's voices to be heard. Otherwise gender differentiated needs in conflict prevention, in peace building and post-conflict relief and rehabilitation are likely to be ignored or subordinated. Feminist scholarly engagements with situations of conflict and peace building in Asia, Latin America, Africa and post Yugoslavia—Europe, have revealed the significance of women as a powerful constituency for peace building and reconciliation.[5]

Present day socio-economic culture is the product of its old feudalistic and new materialistic order. As the increasing rigidity of the caste system meant more control and oppression of women in the earlier days, so now with the deterioration of the law and order situations, crimes against women are on the rise. Women get affected in crucial ways by the decisions at the policy-making levels, by the new changes in the form of modern technology, industry and mining, by the changing social norms etc. Since decisions at the policy level affect women's lives and have a significant impact on them, it is important that more women occupy decision making positions and those who are already there are gender sensitized.

In spite of the constraints women in this region have started coming out of their seclusion and are actively participating in different vocations that were once the monopoly of the males. Their aspirations, perceptions and orientations have been shaped and influenced by the impact of western culture, education, mass media, growing materialism and zeal for self-expressions. Economic hardships and unfavourable socio-economic situations have encouraged many women in North-East to seek employment and pursue their career. There is however a growing realization among some educated women that taking care of their children and serving their husbands are not the ultimate aims of their lives. They can utilize their time and energy in a more productive way, by joining different professional careers.[6]

The structural constraints are felt in the performance of their family roles that are often conflicting with their professional lives. The working women experience a great deal of pressure both at home and in society. The family expectations demand a traditional feminine role. The parent-in-laws and husbands also expect them to be traditional and conservative. Though our society has undergone various changes, parents and husbands who encourage women for career and profession use to think a lot on the suitability of profession for them. Therefore though women have progressive attitude and wider outlook most of them loose interest due to the conservative pressure put by the in-laws and husbands. Such insensibility towards the career motivated women discourages constructive thoughts in them.

But today education is becoming more and more important in the lives of women. Parents are encouraging the children to receive education and sending them to schools and colleges. Today the family is no longer the only institution for deciding their roles. The peer pressure also has come to shape the role and influence personality development of the girls. Besides, industrialization has made continuous shift from family centred to factory centred production. A large number of women have left family located task and have chosen to work in the factory, office, classroom and service establishments. There is now a tacit acceptance of many more women in a variety of professions. Their perception about gender based division has also changed. Nevertheless household work still remains women's responsibility.[7]

Right-based issues with an activist mode against the oppression of the state machinery found in the activist role of the women agencies in some parts of the North-East India including Manipur and Nagaland for example, for restoration of peace and civil liberty and for addressing social issues. These performs provide a space to the women for political activism and struggle for human rights. Although they are yet to cut out a space in the larger political areas, their struggles have shown the potential for emergence of an alternative centre of resistance against the institutional oppression of the state, well outside the traditional power matrix. In other words, such agencies consider the state as the oppressive institution, rather than the patriarchal system that prevails in their societies. We can exemplify the role of women agencies in this connection.[8]

Important issues are thus related to the questions of the position that women have and the rights and privileges they enjoy, their freedom and choice on different matters, access and control of resources and earnings. The answers to these questions would not only suggest this status and position of women in the society but also the problems and constraints they face and how these can be articulated and altered. Thus, despite changes in all such institutions like family, society, economy, education, health, nutrition and politics, the status of women has not improved. The reasons lie in apathy towards women's problems, lack of gender sensitization at the decision making levels, limited member of women in such bodies and the constraints in overall social structures. It is, therefore, essential that those who are sensitive to women's issues enter decision making institutions, in large numbers and work in support with women's and people's movements and organizations. This would require empowerment of women in social, economic and political spheres.

Again, gender in power is found in the emergence of women agencies and women leadership in the North East India focusing on identifying and addressing the strategic gender needs within the framework of patriarchy and reproductive role of women.[9] This idea considered gender as a separate category and indicates the women for all practical purposes.

While the women organizations and women's movement in Manipur has been successful in mitigating socio-political and economic problems and has kept alive the spirit of democracy in the state, it is not without its limitations. They are voluntary in nature. Most of the organizations that represent such movements are without all encompassing rights founded are based on individual or collective enthusiasm for special interests. While such groups may be able to affect small changes, naturally they are limited.

Perhaps the matter of greatest concern is the "gravy train" trend that has accompanied the explosion of civil society organizations in Manipur. Many observers have criticized the inefficiency, and sometimes corruption, associated with different frontal organizations and the support they get. Often, women organizations have proven too small or too inefficient to affect significant changes for the objectives and goals they have mentioned. In that respect, it remains to be seen whether women organizations will continue to command the support and confidence of the people they advocate for, and in turn, remain important elements of the social movements in the state.

The women's movement has been a powerful agent of empowerment and has provided an alternative perspective for fundamental structural changes. The movement has created organizational strength of women, has focused on women's issues and mobilized them around these issues. The women in the movement, however, have shed away from active participation in politics. The women's groups and women's activities thus aim to bring about change in the lives of women and transform it. The women movement and groups have to recognize the importance of women as a constituency and ensure their participation and representation in policy formulation. This can be achieved through reorienting existing structures for entry into decision-making, including political party system and introduce quotas or reservations as a temporary means of women's representation. The movement should also provide a support system (women's groups) for women who enter political processes to win elections. The women's groups working at the grassroots level are small and scattered and have diverse ways of empowering women. There are no infrastructural facilities of networking available that could bring them together and strengthened them while allowing autonomy in their functioning. It is important to create unity in diversity between women's groups, organizations and individuals involved with women empowerment. They need to adopt a common strategy, informed by a common vision to be able to bring about changes in the policies and structures that perpetuate their subordinate status. The issue of political empowerment of women through reservation of seats has been discussed by the leaders of the women movement. They have demanded 30 per cent reservation of seats for women in the grassroots level political institutions, and not 50 per cent as per proportion of women in the population, on the logic that enough women leaders will not be available for filling more than 50 per cent of the total seats in the Panchayati Raj Institutions (PRIs), i.e. about 8 lakh women. Women empowerment in National and State politics has just been a non-starter. Of course, we made a bold beginning in respect of political empowerment of women at the grassroots level during the Rajiv Gandhi regime as during his tenure the Sixty Fourth Constitutional Amendment Bill for reservation for women in Panchayat was introduced. Though it failed in the Rajya Sabha, it was reintroduced in the Narasimha Rao regime. Under pressure from the women's groups, the Government of India passed the 73rd Amendment of the Constitution followed by the 74th Amendment of the Constitution mandating reservation of one-tuird seats for women in all village, block and district level elected bodies. There is also one-third reservation for women in position of Chairpersons and Deputy Chairpersons in these institutions. The provisions have provided great opportunity and challenge to women. Sharing power and responsibilities of the reorganized PRIs with immense control over resources for development and social change will be an empowering instrument for women. The constitutional amendment will definitely bring in at least the stipulated percentage of women in the panchayats. The amendments of the constitution providing reservation of seats is a step forward, and needs to be followed up by necessary changes through land reforms, progressive women's movements and creation of a new culture in time with democracy at the grass-roots level. India is placed in different kind of situation wherein capitalism co-exists with feudalism and nourishes patriarchal values. The patriarchal nature of most of the South Asian countries is shown by Amartya Sen's criteria of 'missing women'. In Manipur, women voters outnumbered male voters in almost all the elections so far. In the Fifteenth Parliamentary Election 2009 the total number of voters in the Outer Parliamentary Constituency of Fifteenth Parliamentary Election 2009 is 4,44,829 male voters while the number of female voters is 4,64,503[10] and in the Inner Manipur Parliamentary Constituency, the total number of voters is 8,26,539 out of which, female voters are 4,34,894.[11]

Due to the paternalistic family and male dominated political structures which do not provide space for women in decision making bodies, women constituted 3.1 per cent of the total contestants in the 1996 election and did not occupy more than 6-10 per cent of the total seats in the state legislative assemblies and parliament. In Manipur only three women have been elected in the State Legislative Assembly. Only one Woman M.P. was elected so far (Kim Gangte). Women's participation in local level political institutions like village panchayats and municipal bodies has also remained insignificant in spite of the government's policy of cooption and reservation of seats for women. Furthermore, women's representation in political decision-making bodies has declined during the past few decades. Chapter 5 of this volume shows the slow progress of Indian women in the participation of political decision-making bodies while it is compared with other countries of the world. The situation is not specific to India but common to the entire South Asian region and the rest of the world.

In recent years, the issues relating to empowerment and advancement of women have gained much attention. The basic objective of women's empowerment is nothing but understanding of one's potential, not only for self-development but also for the benefit of the society as a whole. Women's empowerment is a process of social transformation, where women gain control over resources and benefit and hence influence decisions. It involves five major components such as economic independence, knowledge and awareness, participation, self-image and autonomy.[12] Since women are considered the most oppressed section of the society, the term 'women empowerment' has come to be associated with women's struggle for social justice and equality.

The issue of women's empowerment is central to the achievement of the goals of equality, development and peace, the theme of the Beijing Conference (1995). To achieve these goals, it is essential for women to be in decision-making positions in critical numbers. Furthermore, their entry into decision-making bodies will ensure the restructuring of institutions that are responsible for women's health, sexual harassment and other issues as top priority.

The global data on women parliamentarians prepared by the Inter Parliamentary Union shows that women constitute only 10 per cent of the total membership in parliament. Though the proportion of women in national assemblies is high in Nordic countries and some Socialist countries, women there too do not occupy significant decision making positions within the political structures.

It is through equal participation of women that a transformation in politics can be brought about. It means in all the elections, female voters outnumbered male voters. Politics that shares power equally between men and women and meets women's gender needs will be accountable to people and encourage popular participation. It is important for women to make up within the existing structures to minimize their invisibility, although it is necessary to change the structures also by having space outside of it. Putting women into position of power in public life in a critical number will enable us to bring about changes in traditions more easily.

However, in the present political process of entry into decision-making political institutions, there is growing influence of money and muscle power, backroom dealings, communalization and criminalization. Due to this many women have left political parties and formed informal women's groups. These groups are parts of the women's movement in India.

It is felt that this positive discrimination in favour of women and training of women in exercise of political power will reverse the existing situation among women. Besides, PRIs are an important political innovation and vital conduit in India for popular participation in democratic development.

However, it is one thing for more women to hold political power and quite another to use such power for the required ends. It increased political participation of women has to have any meaning, it should be based on a widespread and well-orchestrated mobilization of women around issues. The elected women representatives must ensure women's empowerment through the political institutions which they represent. Therefore, it is necessary to develop structures and methods for accountability from women representatives and to develop links and support systems between women's groups and the women in political institutions.

The non-partisan women's groups should provide necessary moral and advisory support to women candidates to increase their chances of being elected to political offices. They should work towards enhancing the capacity of women candidates to win the elections by providing them with a forum whereby they could exchange ideas and experiences and learn from experts on electoral laws and politics and evolve issues and strategies to win elections. The orientation programmes should focus on information and training in electoral laws, public speaking, fund rising techniques, resource management and campaign strategies and issues—so that a woman can enhance her chances of winning an election.

In India many organizations of women constituted before and after the Beijing initiatives organized a number of regional or national level conferences on the subject of political empowerment of women. National Alliance of Women (NAWO) organized a conference top draft a manifesto of demands for presentation to the political parties. The manifesto demanded 30-35 per cent reservation for women in state and national level political institutions, and later lobbied for one-third reservation.

With the passage of time and reform movements and the growth of literacy, people came to realize that the development of society ultimately lies in the development and empowerment of women. Hence, many economic and social changes were introduced for women's upliftment, however, the domain of politics was kept out of their reach. It is not that women in the past have not contributed substantially in politics, but because of their secondary status and low esteem, most of them were denied entry in political decision-making.

After independence, women along with men were given the right to vote. The ideas behind this were to accord equal status to women *vis-à-vis* men, and make them politically more aware and active. But much to our distress, the status of women still remains low. Many women do not enter politics because— (1) of widespread exploitation and mudslinging involved; (2) Men are not willing to allow their women colleagues/partners to enter politics, and even entered they are trying to influence and use by male members; (3) Women are still considered to be an object to be possessed by men; (4) Most women do not have the necessary infrastructural facilities and enough money to contest electing women take action to assert themselves as individuals they are bound to be relegated to the background, even though they are performing different activities in connection with the socio-economic and political development of the whole society.

Today North-eastern women participation in outdoor socio-economic activities is gradually increasing. Their participation in social services has also gone up. Greater participation of women in social services encouraged the establishment of various organizations among women. In recent years, the need to involve women in the national development processes has been increasingly recognized. Many women organizations are now working towards achieving this goal, and specific programmes for improving the condition of women have been undertaken by both National and International Agencies.[13]

When women entered into politics, they can certainly make change or transform some conditions of the society.

1. Change their subordinate social and economic status;
2. Change the political structures to a more human perspective towards the interest and well-being of the poor, the children and women and vulnerable sections of society.

3. Remove the current trend of criminalization and communalization of politics.

Women's rights and issues have always been a subject to serious concern for academicians, intelligentsia and policy makers. From pastoral society to contemporary information and global society, the role of women has changed drastically. The role of a typical *'Grihani'* (housewife) who catered to all the requirements of the households including the rearing and upbringing of children in various sub-roles of daughter, daughter-in-law, wife, mother, aunt etc. has been played quite efficiently. The continuity of changes in socio-economic and psycho-cultural aspects of human being has influenced the role of women. With the process of Industrialization, Modernization and Globalization showing its deep impact on the human society all over the world, the role and responsibilities of women have attained new definition perspectives. Further this has also led to addition of responsibility and widened the role of women who also shared the financial responsibilities. Women can share and contribute in all the socio-economic and political activities. But one important thing we need to keep in our mind is gender equality will embody with gender equity. Certain health conditions of women need to acknowledge while they are at their duties. Socio-economic and political empowerment of women will not be meaningful without female health empowerment.

The women issues have received tremendous attention in the planning circle and in wide intellectual discussions and forums at national and global platforms. However, the existing lacuna in the formulation and execution of the policies has not changed the grassroots situation to a great extent. The educational and occupational patterns have also changed and widened with women entering the domains, which till decades back was considered to be dominated by men. Further there has been encouraging rise in the percentage of the women joining service sector especially Banking and Information Technology. In the background of the gigantic transformation, the core issue, which still remains unanswered, is that of women's right and empowerment.

The women's rights are not any exclusive rights as has been debated and put forward patriarchal structure of the society over centuries has gradually led to gender inequality. Women's rights in this context have assumed exclusively. Further when women are not considered equal to the men in the social context the question of women's rights arise. The women's rights are the means by which a dignified living is insured thereby safeguarding her privileges. Thus the basic fundamental rights of speak, freedom and decision-making are her basic rights as an individual and citizen. The right for education and employment are significant for women's development and national development in the wider sense. The power and freedom to exercise these rights is women empowerment. Women's rights and empowerment are not independent to each other. The women empowerment can only be facilitated only if she is able to exercise her rights in the socio-economic spheres of decision-making. As a family is constituted by equal participation of both men and women so is a society, and if any one of them legs behind. It may lead to serious multi-functioning of the society and the system. The women in our society have culturally stagnated and their rights have been denied to them. Though women of today are more thoughtful, more independent, they are still dependent on men in some way or the other, which influences their behavioural pattern. This has led to a feeling of low self-esteem among women. There is a need to make women more aware of their rights, be it social, political or economic. By gaining political rights, they can put a crossed their views among the people and this could lead to a deeper understanding of the problems women face in society. This can be achieved only when more and more women come forward and expose their own cause. Political participation would make a significant difference if it came from those who are at the helm of affairs, and if women are there wielding power—the situation can improve to a great extent and political participation would give every woman a sense of dignity as an individual.

To prohibit and to eliminate discrimination in all its forms and to guarantee the right of everyone, without distinction as to race, colour, or national or ethnic origin, to equality before the law, notably in the enjoyment of the following rights:

(a) The right to security of person and protection by the State against violence or bodily harm, whether inflicted by government officials or by any individual, group or institution;

(b) Political rights, in particular the rights to participate in elections—to vote and to stand for election—on the basis of universal and equal suffrage, to take part in the Government as well as in the conduct of public affairs at any level and to have equal access to public service;

(c) Other civil rights, in particular:

   (i) The right to freedom of movement and residence within the border of the State;

   (ii) The right to leave any country, including one's own, and to return to one's country;

   (iii) The right to nationality;

   (iv) The right to marriage and choice of spouse;

   (v) The right to own property alone as well as in association with others;

   (vi) The right to inherit;

   (vii) The right to freedom of thought, conscience and religion;

   (viii) The right to freedom of opinion and expression;

   (ix) The right to freedom of peaceful assembly and association;

(d) Economic, social and cultural rights, in particular:

(i) The rights to work, to free choice of employment, to just and favourable conditions of work, to protection against unemployment, to equal pay for equal work, to just and favourable remuneration; the right to form and join trade unions;

(ii) The right to housing;

(iii) The right to public health, medical care, social security and social services;

(iv) The right to education and training;

(v) The right to equal participation in cultural activities;

(e) The right of access to any place or service intended for use by the general public, such as transport, hotels, restaurants, cafes, theatres and parks.[14]

Modernity is a product of a number of political, economic and social processes working together in unique historical circumstances. No single 'master process' was sufficient to produce it. For women's emancipation, the consequences of modernization have been paradoxical. In 19th century rationalization of economy and growth of capitalism segregated and genderised the domains of work for men and women separately. Along with genderisation of spheres of economic activities, the rational and emotional capacities of people were also genderised. In this sense modernity created for women precisely the conditions against which feminists have rebelled. Even feminism has provided no unified model for projection of womanhood. The radical trend in feminism has created gender differences as the main principle of feminism. Representatives of this approach like firestone 'went to claim separate fields for women in whom they could develop themselves according to their own principles and potentialities without being hindered by men'. On the other hand challenges are being thrown by media to the constructions of images of feminism in modern global context. The images, styles and models of modernity, created, promoted and projected by the market with the help of technology, are invariably sex-based. It is only co-modified view of women which is being promoted and initiated by women in quest for emancipation. Mass media have taken the role of defining women and symbols of feminism which are invariably independent of reality. The hyper real is the abolition of real not by violent destruction but by its assumptions, elevated to the strength of the model. The tragedy is that images are democratized without democratizing the opportunities and means to realize them in a purposeful way.

On the whole day to day conception of modernity for women remains deeply embedded in sex and symbols and signs related to it. Women are active participants in this image building of theirs. There is need for cultural constructions. The categories constructed as race and gender must be seen as socio-cultural arrangements of roles and identities, because then only we shall be able to decide how we are going to conceptualize the society of ours. Independent of conceptualization of society, formation of categories based on race, gender and class will not help us in understanding emerging technological society of the world.

Globalization is the ultimate and advanced form of capitalism. It is being claimed that under globalization and liberalization, with greater and multidimensional freedom and reliance on market mechanism, would result into empowerment of women but when examine in deep the situation seems otherwise. The present economic philosophy is based upon following premises:

1. All persons are equal and are guided by the profit motive.

2. Everyone has equal opportunity to compete freely to attain his goals.
3. Competition promotes efficiency which is the ultimate source of prosperity and happiness.
4. Market value is important and the values of life need a re-look.
5. An individual knows his interest best and free to pursue it.

The outcome of the above is expansion of multinational companies and invasion on Indian culture. This ultimately reduces person to a commodity which is tradable, including human mind, body, behaviour, desire, relationship and even psyche. With the help of sales promotion measures through modern media, campaigns for commodities mould the mind of the people. Masses are being driven away towards a new world of consumerism. It has resulted into:

1. All persons including women are offering themselves at a price in the market thereby allowing market to exploit them. The market means those persons who possess paying capacity.
2. Since employment of women involves several restrictions by law and in practice too thereby increases the cost of production and makes one uncompetitive, it is natural that lesser women will be employed and thereby their economic independence is reduced drastically or they will have to pay great price for it.
3. Only those women will be preferred who are helping in attracting consumers and here their sexuality and sensuality become important.

All those feminists who support freedom of decision,

making to women are ultimately, in the process, making women disempowered and women is being treated as a piece of beauty for which consumer might be ready to pay a very high price but for the time being. Gender bias in India emanates from the interlocking religious, economic and kinship structures which together define the social domain of men and women. In spite of post-colonial trends of socialism and egalitarian liberalism issues of class, caste and community continue to grip the Indian mind. Social reformers of the 19th and early 20th centuries seem to have been pulled by traditions and customs. Nationalist struggles often seek inspiration from the past and look back to some Indians as the true "National Culture", and all reforms as foreign.

The Constitution is the basic document that reveals the nature and character of the Indian State. While guaranteeing equal protection and equality of law (Article 14) and enacting a non-discrimination clause, the Indian Constitution contains a specific clause for protective discrimination in favour of women and children [Article 15 (1)]. That provision runs [Article 15(3)]:

> "Nothing shall prevent the state from making any special provision for women and children."

Since 1975 which was declared as International Women's Year, and subsequently a decade by the United Nations, a series of studies have provided valuable material on Indian women's rights, 'women's studies' in India have grown both in quality and quantity, but are mostly restricted to a descriptive and symptomatic level. The distinguished sociologist Professor A.R. Desai had perceived a lack of focus and noted "with a sense of sadness" the absence of emphasis on crucial key forces.

Although the number of women voters has increased, no sustained power is accorded to women by this right. If as in some Western countries, their vote is negotiated through what can be called the 'women's agenda', then there can be a form of contract which objectifies the political relationship.

Emphasis has also to be placed on economic rights of women. The link between land ownership and political power in the rural areas needs to be reiterated. Equal rights to women, in both distributed as well as inherited land, have to be ensured. Five decades have passed since the Hindu Succession Act, of 1956 granted Indian women considerable legal rights to inherit immovable property. The Right to Property Act 2005 paid no heed to the tribal population of North East India. Yet most women do not own land, few among those who do are able to control over it. Each lap of the journey, towards legal reforms, from law to the realization of claims, is barricaded by multiple obstacles. Arable land is the most significant form of property in rural areas. It is time to move from single minded emphasis on women's employment by women's organizations to give centrality to women's ownership of land, the means of production itself. As kinship support systems erode, women even from affluent rural households are vulnerable to poverty and destitution.

The United Nations document declaring 1994 as the International Year of the Family has been the subject of criticisms. In the United States, conservative forces such as the New Rights group pointed at the disintegration of the family as responsible for the general deterioration of society. The drug problem was attributed to single mother, for which there are other causes like poverty and unemployment. In India similar sentiments reinforce the patriarchal nuclear family and gender based division of labourer. 'Feminisms' is held to be an anti-family concept as a critique of the existing paradigm of the family with its hierarchical and discriminatory structure has been made by feminists: Alternative models are an imperative if the family is to become the centre of harmony and nurturing as it is intended to be.

The state has to provide them extensive training and work opportunity in the non-farm and rural cottage industries sectors and in the urban informal sectors.

Women have increased sophistication of articulation, clarity of purpose and determined efforts have all combined to take the movement a long way. If women are serious about putting their rights on the national agenda, they have to be uncompromising about their constitutional rights. Placing women's rights in a context gives legitimacy and visibility. Ensuring women's rights creates a basis for a more *humane* society and polity.

In recent years, the issues relating to empowerment and advancement of women have gained much attention. The basic objective of women's is nothing.

The physical and mental violence women experience, and their need to gain respect within their own family and society have been obscured in other politicized issues. Power relations are woven into the social contract of the family. The so called 'abode of peace' can be a site of conflict, violence and insidious abuse of women. The global community has finally begun to acknowledge the extent of violence against women, especially within the family. Such violence is now being called a Human Rights Violation, and fighting such violations is a part of any Human Rights agenda.

NOTES

1. Sarkar, Aanchal, *Gender and Development*, Pragun Publications, New Delhi, 2006, pp.52-53.
2. Amalesh Banergee, 'Women Emancipation and Development, N.E Perspectives', in, Ray B. Dutta and Ray Asok Kumar (ed.), *Women Emancipation, Focus North East India*, Om Publications, New Delhi, 2008, p.261.

3. Amalesh Banergee, 'Women Empowerment and Development', in Ray Basudeb Dutta Ray and Ray Asok Kumar (ed.), *Dynamics of Power Relations in Tribal Societies of North-East India*, Om Publications, New Delhi, 2006. p.134.
4. South Asia Human Rights Documentation Centre, "The Purse Strings as the Noose", *Human Rights Features*, 29 October 1999.
5. Manchanda, Rita. 'The Role of Civil Society in Peace Building', in Fernandes Walter (ed.) *Search for Peace with Justice, Issues Around Conflicts in North East India*, North Eastern Social Research Centre, Guwahati, 2008. p.150.
6. Sengupta, Surojit, 'Career of Women in North East India: An Overview', in Ray Basudeb Dutta and Ray Asok Kumar (ed), *Women Emancipation, Focus North East India*, Om Publications, New Delhi, 2008, p.106.
7. *Ibid*. pp.102-03.
8. Ray, Asok Kumar, 'Traditional Power Structures of North-East India: Some Reflection', in Ray Basudeb Dutta Ray and Ray Asok Kumar, (ed.), *Dynamics of Power Relations in Tribal Societies of North-East India*, Om Publications, New Delhi, 2006, p.108.
9. *Ibid*.
10. *Poknapham* (Manipuri Local Daily), dated, 16-4-2009, p.1
11. *Poknapham* (Manipuri Local Daily), dated, 19-4-2009, p.1.
12. Bhowmik, Krishna, *Indian Women, The Ushering of a New Dawn*, Mittal Publication, New Delhi, 2006, p.IX.
13. Das Paulavi, 'Women Development and Sex Ratio: Treading Between North and North East India', in Ray Asok Kumar and Chakraborty Satyabrata (ed.), *Society, Politics and Development in North East India*, Concept Publishing Company Pvt. Ltd., New Delhi, 2008 p.335.
14. International Convention on the Elimination of all Forms of Racial Discrimination BH490.txt (60 UNTS 195).

APPENDIX-I

List of Women's Organisations which are Actively Working as Pressure Group in Manipur

1. All Manipur Nupi Marup, Imphal West.
2. All Manipur Social Reformer and Development Samaj, Imphal East.
3. Nupi Khunai, Imphal West.
4. Ushoipokpi Tharaorok Women Welfare Association, Lillong.
5. Naga Women's Organisation.
6. Tangkhul Sinaolong, Senapati.
7. Kabui Mother's Association, Imphal East.
8. Kabui Mother's Association, Imphal West.
9. Kuki Women Human Right Network, Churachanpur.
10. Chingmi Tammi Apunba Nupi Lup, Chandel.
11. Kha Nongpok Apunba Nupi Lup Moreh.
12. Manipur University Working Women's Association, Canchipur.
13. Heinoupok Leikai Meira Paibi, Langjing Achouba, Heinoupok.
14. Chaokhat Thourang Meira Paipi, Patsoi.

15. Sri Digambar Jain Mahila Samaj, Paona Bazar.
16. Namdulong Women's Society, Imphal.
17. Sinpham Amasung Saktam Kanba Lup, Khwairamband Bazar, Imphal.
18. Sangaiprou Meira Paibi, Sangaiprou (Kabui), Imphal.
19. Kongpal Lai Hiden Lamjing Meira Paibi, Khurai.
20. Kongpal Kongkham Lainingthou Yangoiningthou Meira Paibi, Khurai.
21. United Tribal Women's Association, Pallel, Chandel District.
22. Kuki Women's Union, Imphal.
23. Kangleipal Muslim Chanura Organisation, Lillong.
24. All Tribal Women's Organisation, Pallel, Chandel District.

APPENDIX -II

Women perform different activities for earning livelihood.

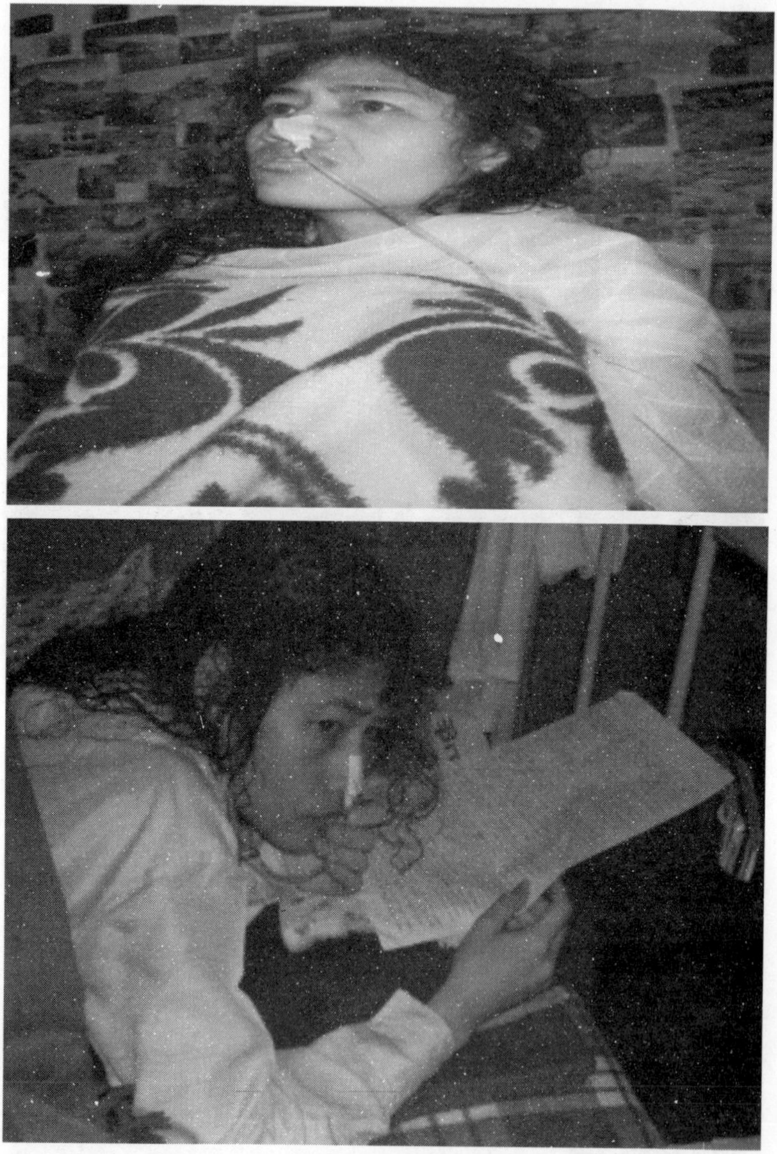

Not only for their own, women are sacrificing their life for the sake of the society. Sharmila, Iron lady launched hunger strike for the removal of AFSPA 1958 since 2000, November.

Nude protest of women against the custodial rape and killing of Thangjam Manorama on 11th July 2004. They have done this by thinking that upon their bodies' women carry the honour of their community and raping them is one of the surest way of defiling the entire community.

Meira Paibi (torch bearer) movement of the Manipuri women.

Women along with different voluntary organisations launched different movements like rally against the different problems created by the governmental and non-governmental agencies which hampered the basic minimum rights of the human beings.

For restoration of peace and normalcy in the society women staged *dharna* and protest movement in a democratic way.

Sandip Panday of Asha Parivar came to Imphal and saluted from Sharmila Chanu for preservation of democracy and human rights

Members of Asha Parivar along with Manipuri women organized sit in protest at Keishampat, Imphal.

The activities of women in Manipur reached the heart of some like minded people of different part of the glove. So they appreciated and gave an award to Sharmila. Sandip Panday of Asha Parivar with his team came at Imphal and saluted Sharmila for preservation of democracy and human rights. They were supported by local NGOs and women groups.

(a) P.I. with Malini Bhattacharya, Member National Women Commission, India and Members of the Women Studies and Research Institute Calcutta University, Kolkata.

(b) P.I. with members of the Kha Nongpok Apunba Nupi Lup, Moreh.

Bibliography

A. *Books*

Aribam Brajakumar Sharma, *Influx of Migrant into Manipur*, Publication Committee, United Committee, Manipur, 2005.

Agrawal, A. P., *Gherao and Industrial Relations*, N.M. Tripathi, Bombay, 1968.

Andal, N. *Women and Indian Society, Option and Constraints*, Rawat Publications, Jaipur.

Carl J. Friedrich, *Constitutional Government and Democracy*, Oxford and IBH, Indian Edition,1966.

Childs, *Public Opinion*, Princeton, D. Von Nostrand, 1965.

Finer Herman, *The Theory and Practice of Modern Government*, Surjeet Publication, Delhi, 1977.

Gokhale, B.K., *A Study of Political Theory*, Himalaya Publishing House.

Ghose, B. N., *Scientific and Social Research*, Sterling Publishers Pvt. Ltd. New Delhi, 1985.

Grahaam Wotton, *Interest Groups*, Englewood Cliffs, New Jersey, Prentice Hall, 1970.

Ghosh, Chitra; Ray, Soma, Chande, Chandni, *Opening the Closed Windows*, Progressive Publishers, Kolkata, 2002.

Johari, J. C., *Comparative Politics*, Sterling Publishers Pvt. Ltd., New Delhi, 1982

Karna, M.N. (ed.), *Social Movements in North East India*, Indus Publishing Company, New Delhi, 1998.

Karam Manimohan Sing, *Nupilal*, K. Premlata Devi, Imphal, 2006.

Kunjakan, K.K., *Feminism and Indian Realities*, Mittal Publication, New Delhi, 2002.

Lal, Dena (ed.), *History of Manipur*, Orbit Publishers and Distributors, New Delhi, 1990.

L. Ibungohal Sing, *An Introduction to Manipur*, Imphal, 1960.

Micheal S. Kimmul, *The Gendered Society*, Oxford University Press, New York, 2000.

MSA Rao (ed.), *Social Movements in India*, Manohar Publication, Delhi, 1984.

Miller, *The Nature of Politics*, Garald Duckworth, London, 1962.

N. Ibobi Sing, *Manipur Administration 1709-1907*, N. Ibetombi Devi, Imphal, 2003.

N. Sanajaoba Sing (ed.), *Manipur Past and Present*, Mittal Publication, Delhi.

Paul R. Brass, *Violence Forms of Collective, Riot, Pogrom, and Genocide in Modern India*, Three Essays Collectives, 2005.

Ray, Asok Kumar and Chakraborty, Satyabrata (ed.), *Society, Politics and Development in North East India*, Concept Publishing Company Pvt. Ltd., New Delhi, 2008.

Roche and Levy, *Parties and Pressure Groups*, New York, Harcourt Brace and World, 1964.

Ray, B. Dutta and Ray, Asok Kumar (ed.), *Dynamics of Power Relations in Tribal Societies of North East India*, Om Publications, New Delhi, 2006.

Ray, B. Dutta and Ray, Asok Kumar (ed.), *Women Emancipation, Focus North East India*, Om Publications, New Delhi, 2008.

Roy, Ashin, *Violence Against Women*, Rajat Publication, New Delhi, 2003.

Sharma, R.N. and Sharma, R. K., *Political Sociology*, Media Promoters and Publishers Pvt. Ltd., Bombay, 1986.

Sarkar, Tanika, *Hindu Wife, Hindu Nation, Community, Religion and Cultural Nationalism*, Permanent Block, Delhi, 2001.

Steward, J.D., *British Pressure Groups, Their Role in Relation to the House of Commons*, Oxford, Clarendom Press, 1958.

Selva Neluka, *The Gendered Nation, Contemporary Writings from South Asia*, Sage Publications, New Delhi, 2004.

Thorner, Alice, Krishnaraj Miethreye, *Ideals, Images and Real Lives*, Sameeksha Trust, 2000.

W. F. Willoughby, *The Government of Modern States*, 1936.

Young, P.V., *Scientific Social Survey and Research*, Prentice Hall Inc., 1962.

Ziegler H., *Interest Groups In American Society*, Englewood Cliffs, New Jersey, Prentice Hall, 1964.

B. Journal, Records, Reports and Megazines

Encyclopedia of Social Sciences.

Annual Report, Gandhi Samriti and Darshan Samiti, New Delhi, 2004-05.

Bharatiya Samajik Chiten, (a quarterly journal of the Indian Academy of Social Services), Indian Academy of Social Sciences, New Delhi.

Economic and Political Weekly, A Samiksha Trust Publication, New Delhi.

Human Development Report 2005, United Nations Development Programme, Oxford University Press, New Delhi, 2005.

International Affairs, Chathan House, New Delhi.

ICSSR, *Newsletter*, New Delhi.

The Indian Journal of Social Works, New Delhi.

Social Scientist, New Delhi.

Third Concept, an International Journal of Ideas, New Delhi.

World Focus (monthly discussion journal), New Delhi.

Office Records, All Manipur Nupi Marup, Imphal.

Office Records, All Manipur Social Reformer and Development Samaj, Imphal.

Office Records, Ushoipokpi Tharaorok Women's Association.

Office Records, Manipur University Working Women's Association.

Office Records, Kha Nongpok Apunba Nupi Lup.

C. Papers (National and Local)

I. National Papers

Amrita Bazar Patrika, Kolkata.

The Hindu, New Delhi.

The Hindustan Times, New Delhi.

The Indian Express, New Delhi.

The Statesman, Kolkata.

The Times of India, North East, Guwahati.

The Telegraph, Kolkata.

II. Local Papers

Huyen Lanpao (Manipuri daily), Imphal.

Prajatantra (Manipuri local daily), Imphal.

Poknapham (Manipuri local daily), Imphal.

Sangai Express (English daily local paper), Imphal.

Sangai Express (Manipuri local daily), Imphal.

Index